For those who have met the G
who have y

Pictures from the King
Small Collection
2009-2016

Introducing Jess - The Vision Bearer

Written by

Simone Shaw

A Publication for Torchlight Ministry
No part of this book may be copied or reproduced without prior consent of the author
2017 COPYRIGHT ©
ISBN-13:978-1536974713
ISBN-10:1536974714

Transformation is available through My Spirit,
and all who submit to Me
Will experience this transformation in
themselves.

You are a new creation
Old things have passed away
Behold all things have become new.

Contents

Dedication

For my family. My wonderful Mum and Dad, my beautiful daughter Amber and my brothers Mark, Louis and Robert - treasures in the darkness. My dear friends Alan and Hazel have been an inspiration; they have my most sincere gratitude for the time they spent mentoring and growing me as a young Christian.

It is my deepest desire that this first collection will be like treasures in the darkness that people can pull out as they wish. I pray for hope and much blessing in the lives of all who read it.

Acknowledgements:
Cover design: Mike Coomber, New Forest House of Prayer UK
A great deal of the inner healing and deeper roots of understanding; reflected in these accounts, have come about by the healing ministry, teaching and love for God I received from ELELL Ministries and it is with great thanks and eternal gratitude I acknowledge God's wonderful work.

Foreword

When Simone and I first connected through my ministry, I immediately recognized her unwavering, eternal love for Jesus Christ and His everlasting kingdom. As our paths continued to intersect, it also became very clear about Simone's strong bond and love for all of mankind, including God's people and heritage, the Jewish people and the Promised Land of Israel. So, for someone who holds the same beliefs and convictions, once Simone told me that she was writing a book, I was very excited to read her work.

In her book, Pictures from the King, Simone reveals a fascinating collection of inspirational and Biblical truth, as she journeys through her encouraging personal story. Through Simone's trials and tribulations, dreams and visions, and her reference to wonderful biblical accounts of God's sovereign, righteous, and divine ways, she conveys an incredible picture of God's everlasting love for all of His remnant, including you and me!

Additionally, with Simone's intimate encounters throughout her life with the Almighty, which includes her own unique testimony and documented journal entries, she totally inspires a believer or a non-believer to seek the Lord God with all of their heart, soul, mind, and strength, so that they can truly find ultimate peace through Him and understand His majestic ways.

After reading and comprehending Pictures from the King, you will be able to recognize God's amazing characteristics, ways, and attributes on how He persistently works on believers and non-believers alike, calling all to salvation through Jesus Christ. You will also be able to truly appreciate God's right Hand, Jesus Christ, in your life and also in the lives of others. Pictures from the King is a great testimony that is grounded in Biblical truths that will inspire you to find your treasures in darkness.

Chadwick Harvey, author of God's Prophetic Timeline,
Messiah's Final Warning

Introduction

My *'small collection series'* tell the story of a long journey with the Great King; Jesus Christ.   Charting a passage that reflects transformation and miraculous testimony. Our lives will provoke many conflicts as we journey and will be embraced by our faith but juxtaposed are the awesome, mind blowing encounters we meet in knowing God.

However this Journey is also a depiction of a struggle. Nobody receiving Christ and starting out on the narrow path can avoid confrontation with oneself and with God.   Yet it becomes the struggle that defines us.   People often ask "What about suffering, if there is a God why do people suffer?" I cannot answer these questions in extreme cases but I do know that our individual walk with God is   a pathway of joy and thanksgiving but also affliction, as Christ Himself was our pattern.   The struggle is vital to shaping us and to who we will eventually become; *Christ-like,* and that *is* the prize.
Whether you know Jesus or not, you too can find Him in all His glory, learning to trust the special purpose He will have planned for your individual life.

Jess entered the still, small space. The little square partition. In front of her was the King. He had come as Shepherd. Looking up she realised she could see passed Him. He turned to indicate the great pastures in the distance. Turning she saw a large, open green field with many, many sheep. Looking now to the Shepherd, the pastures fading, the partition became a garden. She knew He was calling her into His garden to sit awhile, to breathe Him in, to inhale restoration. All about Him was peace. She observed a bench - probably beautiful, ornate but the details were hazy, irrelevant as she soaked in the colour and fragrance of the garden. Hanging, trailing flowers, quickly fading as her gaze returned to the Shepherd. In a flash she saw His sovereignty, the Great King, beautiful beyond description, eyes violet, large and penetrating, wonderful unison of Spirit pulling her towards His gaze. A perfect trust a desire to know and be known, far above all comprehension and yet a rest that encompassed eons of time. He knew her. Now He stood in His field, swishing long, ripe sheaves of wheat with His hands, a beautiful movement as He brushed the wheat towards her indicating her own harvest to come. Thank You her heart whispered unable to open her mouth and then He spoke, "sit with Me. I will equip you, I will provide for your every need." His words sent waves of breathless, powerful seas, into gushing oceans deep with His love, deep with the promise of peace in the next traversing of her journey.

The Butterfly Encounter

Brief Encounter

It is said that the darkest time of night is just before the dawn. Apparently that last hour that leads to the breaking of day is the darkest of all. This is so like life. Many times we go through what seems our deepest trial when for some inexplicable reason our life begins to turn around for the better. When we allow Jesus to enter our hearts and give Him Lordship over His wonderful purpose and plan for us we become more aware that these times of trial and testing are times of polishing and refining. This forces us closer to Him until He becomes our all sufficiency.

But when we don't yet know Him or His love and grace it may seem as though there is no way out of these dark times. God once told me that people who have been in a dark place for a very long time believe they will never get out. I guess this is why people sink into depression and unhappiness, even becoming suicidal. Well here is a glimpse of the light of Christ being revealed to me during an extremely unhappy, low period in my life. I felt very lost and completely alone. My beautiful daughter was very young possibly three years old and we were walking around a regular little walk by a lovely stretch of beach. As a mum we hide these feelings as much as we can showing strength for our children. I have to say my daughter has always carried a light and wisdom beyond her years and is another shining light in my life, bringing great joy. Anyway it was *our* beach. Here my daughter would take the same little trails such as walking along the side of a narrow wall, jumping over mooring posts and climbing a big, black anchor whilst I walked alongside her and joined in at varying intervals.

There is something very peaceful and refreshing about the sea especially when you have the added beauty of boats moored along the jetties and wonderful views around the coast. This particular day, I sat down on the ground looking out to sea whilst my daughter played alongside me. In contrast to the beauty around me the feelings of loss and desperation were like a darkness within, a hidden place. Yet God knew my inner being and out of nowhere I became very aware of the presence of an angel who subsequently bent down and hugged me. I still know to this day it was an angel of God, sent by God. I had the most tremendous sense of peace that undoubtedly follows His presence. That peace is our witness. I thank my God for that wonderful gift with all my heart and all I have to give. I had done nothing to deserve anything. Yet that is the wonder of God. We are His children and He loves us and He chose this opportunity to give me a glimpse of that love. This very dark period in my life was just before the dawning of my salvation in Jesus.

By the way of the sea beyond the Jordan. The people who sat in darkness have seen a great light...*Isaiah 9:2*

Encounter

Some years back I was in my flat when out of nowhere a butterfly landed on the carpet. Not being overly keen on insects I crept towards it cautiously and slowly. I sat down on the floor and felt strangely intrigued by it. For some reason it did not flutter or move away as I came close but sat still with its wings closed. It was a white, cabbage butterfly and instinctively and very unusually for me I touched the tip of its wings. The wings simply fell open. In exactly the same manner, I simultaneously saw the pages of a Bible fall open as the words "Seek and you shall find," passed straight through my mind. In time, I was to discover these words were actually *in* the Bible. Did I know it was God's voice at that time? I think I did. Had *you* known me at that time; my life being wild and reckless, it may seem surprising that God would speak to me at all, but you would also begin to understand how God loves us all and is interested in every one of us, just as we are.

On reflection I cannot for the life of me recall what happened to the butterfly yet I *knew* I'd heard God's voice. With my whole being, I *knew* it had happened. Moreover I have no idea why God used a simple butterfly to reach me but in so many ways since knowing God, my life has become more and more free, which is greatly symbolic. I once heard that when people *dream* of butterflies it is supposed to characterise hope which is just what God has given me and is now manifesting through me to others. God has continued to reveal Himself to me in remarkable ways. The truth is He loves us and is always drawing us to Himself.

If you are reading this book I suspect He may be drawing *you.*

Since this remarkable encounter I have met many people who have had momentous encounters with God but for most people it has been a *gradual* realisation of salvation and His truth and presence. This same God created us all uniquely and *reaches* us all individually. The Psalms depict that God has fashioned our hearts individually; the deepest part of us that reflects who we truly are.   Yet subsequent to my wonderful encounter I am now empowered to share with such conviction, the wonders of God and to encourage you to seek encounter for yourselves. He *will* reveal Himself to you. He promises *"Seek and you shall find."*

Nevertheless we all come in different ways. A butterfly may not land on your carpet but God will know how to reach *you*. It may happen that His presence will be revealed within ever expanding revelations as you become increasingly aware of Him and start seeing your purpose unfold before you. God says He was found by those that did not seek Him. Simply call on Him but keep pressing in, believing. Remember He is seeking *you.* He is using me right now like that butterfly, in just the same way. One day He may use you to reach others. Life will not suddenly become perfect or easy.   In fact the road is rocky and tough but the road leads to life - eternal life. What an exciting journey? You will *know* where you are going when you die and you will go from strength to strength.   No matter how precious your life appears just now, nothing compares to knowing the truth, the real God of the Bible who died for us to make a way.

"For God so loved the world that He <u>gave</u> His only begotten Son *Jesus* that whoever believes in Him should not perish but have everlasting life."
John 3:16

This is a promise and it is the truth.

A few years before my butterfly encounter I was walking along with a friend, arguing with them vehemently that their belief in God was founded purely on a fear of going to hell and was therefore unreasonable.   For some reason I could not accept their faith and found it made me irritated and angry. Yet deep down in the secret place I *knew* there was a God, even before my butterfly experience, something deep within had always known there was a God, but I could not admit it at this time. I also could not understand it. I don't know why. Perhaps I had always been so used to living out the front everybody else did that I was afraid to admit the truth. Even as a young girl I could remember asking people if they believed in God, because I *knew* I did.

I often felt I could see a picture of an old man in the sky sitting on a cloud far away. As a young girl perhaps this image was right for my age and understanding. A bit like those wonderful pictures we draw as children with a line of blue sky, a big sun and perhaps a house or a smiling person. The flowers we draw are probably as big as the house and the trees reach to the sky. It is because our perspective is different. Yet God knows what we are able to receive or understand at any given time. After all it is Him who made us, we are His creation and He designed our walk through life to be gradual, interesting and complex. Life is a mystery that we discover, growing ever more intimate with time. Whenever we have anything in life too quickly it destroys itself and often a part of ourselves with it. It is *His* heartbeat we are to be in tune with.

"In Him we live and move and have our being." Acts 17:28.

The Bible states that creation itself declares that there is a God and that He knows everything about us.   So I do not know why I should argue so passionately this day or deny God's existence so intensely, only that there was a warring inside me, a struggle to believe the truth. Or more aptly to admit that I believed it. With the butterfly encounter yet to be uncovered, I had an unexpected journey ahead.

Nevertheless my friend presented an interesting challenge. He said:

"One day when you are alone, ask God to show you - the

way, the truth and the life."

I said "Ok."
If I am honest deep down I was excited, I had unconsciously seen the dramatic change in my friend's life and was touched somewhere by their transformation and utter conviction about God.

It was during a lunch break from work when I decided I would do it, put it to the test. I went to a little park alone, sat down, got out my sandwiches and looked up declaring:

"Ok show me the way, the truth and the life."

I can only describe what happened next as automatic, because without knowing why, I unconsciously got up, packed up my lunch left the park and walked around the corner straight into a small charity shop. There in front of me on a glass shelf, standing upright, was a Bible! A little, blue Bible right in front of my eyes. I thought,
 "No way!"

 I bought the Bible and kept it for many years but never read it - feeling it somehow protected me.
"Ask and you will receive." Matthew 7:7

Some years later I became involved in alternative therapies. Although I'd had these amazing experiences of God there was a sense of fragmentation in my life. The composites had not quite gelled and there was nothing solid that I could mesh together. No sense of identity or belongingness just a grappling for the truth. If you can imagine at conception, a cell dividing and collating with other cells to form a person. As the corresponding cells connect one can imagine a spark igniting as they link and clump together with one accord. There is a unison, as with a magnet when shards of metal are abruptly and sharply pulled upwards. Yet when all the pieces are pulling in opposite directions there is no interlocking framework to connect them together.   I was looking in all the wrong places dabbling in healing arts which were a million miles away from the truth but I *was* seeking.

This particular day I was laying hands on someone doing Reiki healing...

Reiki is a deception and does not originate from God. I would strongly deter anyone from dabbling in this art - the origins are extremely dubious. Reiki comes from a very dark place - the devil will disguise himself as an angel of light. There is only one truth, one light and that is Jesus Christ, as I was just about to find out.

...during this moment as my hands were stretched out before me on someone's head I felt the hand of Jesus Christ placed completely inside my own hand. I stood absolutely still, frozen in time but sensing a complete peace. I was utterly astonished but incredibly moved. The experience was so real there are no meaningful words to describe it. I also knew it was outside of everything I was doing, an interception and that He was the true healer, even though I didn't really understand this. Here again, I was being shown the truth; another way. Jesus had revealed Himself to me again. Somehow this time, there was a knowing inside of me that I could not quite explain, only that something truly remarkable had happened. I can only say that this time I *knew* it was Jesus Christ. I still did not know *who* He actually was but I knew it was Him. It was the butterfly encounter all over again. I did know Jesus hung on a cross but I didn't know why. It may sound naïve but I had never really been to church in my life and had never been taught anything about Him - why would I? My family were yet unsaved. Yet here was the hand of Jesus Christ being placed right inside mine. For several days it chipped away at me. To say I was in shock is such an incredible understatement. I was in fact completely and utterly driven. Who was this Jesus? Why did He put His hand in mine?

Around this time I was launching an alternative healing clinic with a friend and for some reason it never got off the ground. Co-incidentally, for some even greater reason didn't ever got going at all!

The hand of God?

Well very shortly afterwards I went to see my friend to share my miracle and was so enraptured with my experience that I could not stop talking about it. It really affected me and I had to know why. I talked for some time about it. In fact over and over, I just couldn't let it go. I seemed to be experiencing a heightened sense of life and began for example to recollect and discuss with her a book I was writing. It suddenly became very important. It was completely ungodly in the sense that it was a fictitious account of two people that were reincarnated and had met again in this lifetime. Although the book had these erroneous elements it also fantasised about the spirit world where light and dark were a reality and that good and evil spirits were operating through people and causing the world to be in the state it was. I was also just about to find out this was indeed a reality. Dark forces *do* work in the world and through people to bring about destruction and the Holy Spirit does work through those who receive Him to demonstrate His goodness through them. I believe God was revealing things to me even in the darkness before I understood who He was. Yet needless to say it wasn't long before I ditched the book.

Earlier that afternoon, I had been very attracted to a tiny picture of a cross but still did not understand it all. God was drawing me, ever closer.

Over and over I tried to comprehend it as I kept sharing my experience when I suddenly became aware of who Jesus was - that He was God.

This really was a knowing deep within the depths of my being, a sense of deep exposure accompanied by an awesome wonder and fear. I was colliding with truth. At this point we were sitting opposite each other in arm chairs and I was becoming increasingly aware of a presence moving in closely behind me, the deep presence of something very holy - Almighty God. I felt intensely afraid and yet the most incredible peace. I found myself confessing that Jesus was God and immediately my eyes were opened! The moment I said those words God passed through my whole body just as light, and I felt myself being transported back through my life especially times of trauma and difficulty. I could feel every cell in my body being stretched and altered as I was taken back through my life. I cried deep tears of healing and realisation. It was the most profound and sincere moment of my life. I looked to my friend and declared,

"I'm born again..."
I did not understand the true implication of this statement only that I had encountered God and that His name was Jesus. My life had been changed in an instant. I had in fact entered another whole dimension, God's kingdom. It was a total revelation. My life never returned to its former meaning. Instead it took on a radical; yet measured and utter transformation.

...Remarkably I still had a cigarette in one hand and a glass of wine in the other which seemed really fixed and utterly magnified in my hands. I was still incredibly shaken by what was happening to me and did not realise at the time that the reality of Jesus was being revealed to me by the Holy Spirit; who brings us to the truth of God and had been resting right behind me and had in fact passed right through me.

When the Helper comes, whom I shall send to you from the Father, the Spirit of truth who proceeds from the Father, He will testify of Me. John 15: 26

During this mind blowing and rather tearful encounter I looked in front of me and saw a light shining like the sun - its rays pouring out and radiating upwards just like a bright, white sun. Another light began to pass around me like a figure of eight going around the two of us. I can only say that I was taken to another place whilst sitting in that chair. Now the whole room was full of light and I found myself speaking out of my mouth again that Jesus was God. Again my eyes were opened and I saw two angels sitting behind my friend, but they were dark and I felt fearful of them. I could see them clearly. I had not realised that angels could be dark. It was as though something had been removed from my eyes and I could suddenly see the things of the spirit as they really were. If I could describe how I felt at this point it would be like being caught up in God's Spirit, in His hands, becoming a part of who He really is and seeing things as I had never seen them before. As they really are, in the Spirit. Although I was acutely aware of the scale of things I still felt a tremendous peace. I knew I had found truth. The very thing I was looking for, real truth. I may not have fully grasped it all, but no matter, God had been leading me for many years. He never gives up on us...

Now I understand why Jesus is the Shepherd who gives life to His sheep - those that will respond to His call, because you see, we think we choose Him but He has chosen us and He has chosen us to reveal Him to others.

...I then saw a line, a straight, visual line in front of my eyes - a dividing line and on the left of that line was every occult practice I was undertaking. All the alternative therapies and practices such as Tarot and crystals - everything. At the time I did not know these things were dark and occult (even though I was afraid of them) I just thought I was investigating the spirit world which I was, but unfortunately the dark side. This is a very serious thing and never to be taken lightly. On the right side of the line I saw a Bible and a cross. I clearly saw these things and I knew I was being given a choice. God in all His grace and glory and beautiful peace showed me the truth with His wonderful dividing line. I chose that right side and have never ever wanted to go back to any 'alternative' practice.

My eyes are opened now and my life belongs to Christ, my true life is hidden with Him until I enter eternity. As it will be for all those who accept His free gift of life. I had crossed a line from this life into eternity, never to return.

Another unfolding aspect of my experience is that my eyes were more and more opened to the wine and cigarette I held. This remains an essential element of my encounter. Although this moment was monumental and so much happened it *was* only a moment as my cigarette was still in my hand! But I had entered eternity and time could not be measured there.

I could see the harm cigarettes were doing to me and there is nothing wrong with wine in itself but it was my lifestyle that was wrong and God was opening me up to this. However it was a little way down the line before I stopped smoking. Probably a few months after this encounter I developed a hacking cough and wanted so badly to give up. Well here is another miracle of God. I was lying in bed and I could not stop coughing. In fact I believe with my whole heart I was seriously ill. I would crawl out of bed, go down stairs, drink pints of water, come back to bed and have to drink more. I walked around like an old lady coughing and wheezing and feeling that I could cough no more. When suddenly I reached out to God.

The Bible tells us, "Draw near to Me and I will draw near to you." James 4:8
Calling out from my heart I promised Him if He would help me that night I would never smoke again. I had smoked for a life time being completely and utterly addicted. Well I really felt that I might die but instead I just remember going to sleep and waking in the morning completely healed. I had no desire to smoke.

A short time after this I kept going passed a little church close by my house. I knew that one day I would go in there. I had no idea what it was about, just that I would go there. Jesus opened my eyes to that church and I was very drawn to it. The following Christmas a leaflet advertising a nativity play came through my door. I remember saying to my daughter "we are going to church tonight" and feeling so excited about it. This is where I met other wonderful Christians and came to understand more and more of my experience and the Bible. I will always be thankful to the faithful people of God who mentored and supported me. Even though I still experienced difficulties and had a long way to go in terms of internal restoration and healing in God, the Christians I encountered were caring and understanding. This is not how I would describe myself at this time but coming out of the world and into church and God's world is a life transition, developing and shifting over time. They were just as patient as God had been in His pursuit of me. So whilst I certainly have not always been the person God has formed in me now - becoming slowly more Christ-like, they helped my journey immeasurably.

"Let your light so shine before men that they may see your good works and glorify your Father in heaven."
Matt 5:16

Metaphor

Gazing ahead, her eyes absently fixated, Jess toyed with the key. Turning it quickly and repeatedly through her fingers, she enjoyed the intensity of the motion. She felt the thrill of the rhythm.   Such as catching something unexpectedly
in mid air; a ball, a piece of paper, a fresh revelation! The satisfaction of holding it in your hand, of having caught it. Yet almost immediately she became irritated by the key; its lack of grit. It was another fake. It spoke for itself. They all had. She threw open the window, breathing in great lung's full of night air she reflected over her life. The dark sky had taken on a clarity, a crispness, stars glinting. As she pushed the window back further, memories of her life flooded back. In her youth she had often stood by her bedroom window, late into the night, the same stars blazing, offering a glint of freedom by their sheer volume and distance. Could they be reached? Cigarette in hand she would watch the hot ash falling, like a tiny fire ball; exploding into a thousand little stars as it crashed the floor outside. She no longer yearned in this way for freedom but she yearned for truth. Her mind flooded back. She remembered arguing with her father as they had walked and talked through her childhood town where

the bustling city seemed very far away from this remote place. She remembered how critical she'd been of his new found faith but deep down she had known it was true. There _was_ a God but she could not, would not admit it. Was it a blindness, a stubbornness of spirit? She had no idea.

A cool breeze interrupted this flow of thought and Jess abruptly closed the window. Glancing once more at the night sky she seemed to momentarily attain a sense of completion, the endlessness of eternity.

Lately she had taken to an exploration of reality; what was life about, was this all there was? She had encountered some experiences albeit dark and frightening and within alarming proportions but she knew there was more, where was the truth of life?

It was as though her whole world had been reduced to a room now and its population to one. In the room, was a Door, obscured from view but no less a Door. In the middle of the room, a box. A huge, curious, age – old box full to the brim with keys.   The room had developed a longing in her to escape from the superficiality of life. Yet life had somehow taken on a newness, a depth of meaning, a desire above all things to find the truth. She knew there was more.

She began rifling through the box of keys. An activity that progressed to days, months and finally years. Some of the keys she kept in her hands for years consumed by their luminosity, their intrigue. Time after time turning them over and over in her hands. It was hard to let go, they carried such an indefinable quality about them. Some she ignored, some she dismissed, others bored her. Yet some of them had a deep magnetism almost demanding her to consider and reconsider their worth. They dwelt in her hands like gold dust or indelible ink. Some were really attractive tasting of exotic fruit or reflective like colourful sweets, but always they would lose their intensity especially as she continually became aware of other keys; even more mysterious keys. Yet somehow, over time the keys appeared to fade from their former glory into a dark glow. She sensed something new was drawing her. Quite suddenly the keys seemed to disappear and wilt as an intense chink of light could be seen in the box, just a faint spark but how bright it was. Then suddenly it was in her hand. It was different from all of the other keys, it fit. In her palm it held a reality, a truth, a safety. Like coming home or holding the hand of Almighty God. As she clasped it tightly a knowing filled her very being. This was it! She knew without any doubt this was the key. Walking quickly, swiftly to the Door, she hurriedly placed it in the lock and of course it fit! ...

...Jess turned the lock and pushed open the Door she caught a glimpse of the King; the purity of His light threw her to her knees. There was no turning back.

As she walked through the Door and continued towards the light she was being renewed, old things were passing away, a hand was guiding her, her heart fully at peace. As she continued on she felt a helmet being placed on her head.   An awareness grew inside her, someone was squeezing her very heart. She began to think about others still trapped in lies and deceit. The Door had closed behind her but she must go back, she couldn't leave them. Her heart moved with compassion.   She must tell them – the real key was within them, its name Repentance. The Door would always open with the correct key. She must bring them out of darkness and into this glorious light but how would they know if she didn't tell them and how would they know if she didn't return? She felt the hand guiding her once more, a still, small voice saying, "Go."
Her mind resolute, this had now become a decision. The decision had now returned with a promise. The promise would live on inside her forevermore and was taking the form of treasure; that pearl of great price becoming more and more valuable the more it is passed on. The treasure had become a kingdom within. The kingdom brought with it authority.   Yes an authority over the other keys!   No longer would they confuse, trick or delay her because

within this kingdom lay discernment. Looking up she realised the helmet had a name - 'Salvation.' In her hand appeared a sword a great swishing sword that took the form of words,   the truth wielding the power of those words, the expressions of God's truth. It cut through the air like precious steel. Even at a distance as she drew that sword she felt the *other keys* push down inside their box, fearful, they hid like frightened crickets, but silent. She held the key in her hand tightly, but she knew it was really the Door that had mattered. She knew she had needed to desire that Door with all her heart to find the right key.

Jess smiled, the smile of a conqueror. "Here." she would say. "I have the key. It is a simple key, one that brings a gift of life and freedom. A freedom that can never be lost or stolen."   In her heart a joy inexpressible that she yearned to share and pass on. She had a very long journey ahead but no matter the Door would never be closed to her and maybe, just perchance others would cross that beautiful threshold with her

Jesus says: "I am the door if anyone enters by me he will be saved and will go in and out and find pasture."
John 10:9.
"I am the way, the truth and the life, no one comes to the Father except through Me." John 14:6

If you desire to know the real person of Jesus, ask Him.

The Race

Closing her eyes Jess ventured to find Him. Her heart whispered prayers stilling the fears within.   Softly she spoke in earnest aspiration esteeming Him faithful. Father please send Your angels to guard us. Then closing her eyes once more she saw, filling the room, filling the house, filling the garden... white, beautiful, a purity of light and goodness that no evil could surpass. Her words became lost in expressions of delight as once more her King arrived. Jesus You came, how beautiful You are. Those eyes, the eyes of kindness of gentleness of a beauty that knows no bounds. How they seemed to bore into her very being. Absorbing, encompassing every thought and yearning of her heart, impressing deep sensations of heaven into her soul; united in eternity with the Warrior King.

Our times in God's hands

For some time Jesus has been showing me a picture of a chariot. I am sat in the chariot with Him, He is holding the reigns. We are about to embark on a fast journey. He is going to do a new thing and I need to be ready. Yet nothing happens, time rolls on and I press in, I pray but our situation stays the same.

Now I see a dark tunnel. It is not gloomy because it is gradually getting lighter. I am in a fast train whizzing through this tunnel at great speed. As it bursts out into the light it keeps going, on and on. Chug, chug, chug. Seemingly on a never ending journey. I can see the mountains up ahead, a long way off. Will I ever get there? Suddenly the train stops; or is it a chariot, beside the mountain? There is a long pathway up to the summit. It is long, windy and disappears into the distance. Jesus is at the top He is calling to me, full of joy. The summit is green and sheep are feeding, only sheep no goats. Jesus is beckoning and pointing to a further mountain with another winding stairway to the top. The journey is His. Trust is vital. He has gone before and He is waiting up ahead. Everything has a time and a purpose. A time to be born and a time to die. When we become soaked in His presence we begin to see how our lives tie together and connect - we cannot see the links at the time, we are just treading the water.

In the same way God wants to use us where we are, right now. The road is set before us and our purpose established. The paths are sequential but not fixed, they are already formed but we can choose which way we go. We just need to submit each day and listen and trust in what we hear and feel in Him. If I had not gone to a certain friend's house 'by 'chance' one day she would not have offered me a job, if she had not offered me a job, I would not have met my daughter's dad, would not have had my daughter or moved to Gosport or met God in the way I did, in His perfect timing. Even when I did not know God; completely immersed in the way of the world, He worked everything together for good until the perfect time when I would collide with Him. God has been with me my whole life. If we are His, He will have His hand on our lives even when we are still in the darkness and will keep us alive for His future glory.   All things do work together for good. As such; many years ago, my friend and I were hitchhiking in France, yes we were young and incredibly foolish:

Relieved to have a lift on this hot summer's day we bundled our bags in to the back of the little French car and both climbed in.   As the road rolled on I glanced around me inadvertently noticing that the back doors had no handles and the doors were seemingly jammed shut. It occurred to me in passing, that if I needed to get out of the car I would be trapped. Continuing to look around I now noticed our friendly driver looked incredibly huge so much so that his neck was bent over and it was crammed into the space above him. Was he a giant! I began to feel concerned when only a short distance into the journey I heard my friend shouting loudly at the driver, "Stop the car, stop the car!" Immediately I felt overcome with fear and asked her what was happening. In my limited view; surrounded by bags, I hadn't realised the man's behaviour had become dangerous and threatening. My friend continued to shout and I began to exclaim that I may be trapped in the back. I lunged forward in my fear only to be thrown backwards by the giant. What had we done? Reality struck as we knew we were deeply in trouble when for some inexplicable reason the driver stopped. However he continued to terrorise my friend. Yet seemingly; as within a millisecond, the unexpected stop gave her a small window of opportunity; with lightening genius she grabbed the keys from the dash, cracked open the door and ran at breakneck speed up the road. The giant tore out of the car and gave chase to get his precious keys giving me time to get out of the car just as my friend was on a speedy circuit back.   Providentially as he snatched back the keys he hurled our bags out of the car and sped off. When it comes to life or death possessions have no meaning but it was good to get back our money and passports. He drove off laughing as we stood bewildered, big lesson learnt.

I will always be thankful to my friend for potentially saving me from harm or death but was it really God's hand and His angels presiding over us? We did not know Him at this time but did He know us? My friend had no spiritual weapons of warfare, no understanding of the power of the kingdom but God saved us. It seems to be the case that if someone is backed right into a corner or faced with death they may effect their only available action and pray - 'God help me!' Thankfully we don't have to be backed into a corner or terrified to call on Him but it is remarkable how we do, when we don't even know if we believe! It still amazes me that God has done miracles throughout my family which at this point they may not even recognise as such but praise God they will.

One evening, in their youth, my mother and her friend accepted a lift from a stranger in a beautiful car, (some kind of generational irrationality in personal safety presiding here!) However on stepping into the car my mother realised that she could not get in and consequently her arm was literally thrown off of the door. My mother is hard of hearing and perhaps it is true that God gives us extra gifts of discernment when we are lacking in one of the physical senses. She just could not enter the car and refused the lift, much to the annoyance of her friend. When the car drove off they continued to walk over a bridge where on passing they saw the wreck of the beautiful car jammed into the railings at the side of the bridge. God's hand?

My father also experienced a great miracle before knowing Christ. He was driving along one day and for some reason lost control of the steering. I believe there was gravel on the ground and he began to skid; completely losing a grip on the wheel, when someone took hold of his hands and placed them firmly on the steering wheel helping him to manoeuvre to safety. He was in fact alone in the car.

My brother, as a little boy would frequently attempt to jump from the top of the stairs to the bottom. One particular day as he jumped he was lifted up and carried to the bottom of the stairs by an unknown company. God says He will guard us with His angels and this would appear to be true. In my estimation God must have His hand on my brother's life whether he realises it or not just now. Does God give us these clues in the hope we will turn from ourselves and into His arms?

He certainly knows the beginning from the end.

The Bible also reveals the way God is working through times, people and circumstances to bring about His perfect will. In the book of Genesis Judah the son of Jacob slept with his daughter in law; believing she was a prostitute he had no idea that this would maintain the generational line for our precious Lord Jesus to enter the world? Through others' weaknesses, sins and mistakes all the way down the line to Jesus. Only Jesus is perfect, only He is God. When He walked as a Man on earth, He did not sin or make mistakes but He turns all of ours to good if we will trust in Him and give Him a true place within us then He can express and demonstrate this wonderful mystery through us.

What's around the corner?

With great joy I enter the side of the empty house. I am young possibly nine and the world holds great, unknown adventure. I pass through the gate, slinking down the side of the garden, marvelling at this overgrown jungle. Coming around the back of the house I seem to be aware of the presence of much glass. Was it a conservatory, was the house so huge and its windows so big that they dazzled my perception? Turning in now through the back entrance I am aware of greenery growing under my feet, there is debris, broken glass and tiles are strewn about the floor. Yet I am drawn upwards as the sparkling sunshine cascades colour through the numerous windows. It is summer, I am happy. I glide from room to room, drifting in and out of my own Narnia; a house full of expectation and fantasy. I climb the stairs aware of the excitement of being completely alone in this great house. I drift into an upstairs bedroom and soak in the atmosphere. Unconsciously I am in the front bedroom now and suddenly aware I no longer feel alone. On the floor is a bed, an old mattress with a sleeping bag. There is a small gas stove and signs of life; boots, paper. Terrified I turn on my heels, heart racing and pounding in my chest. I run like lightening down the stairs and can't wait to get out of the house that I had longed to be in. Who was it? Would they jump out? Were they watching me?

Looking back I probably cut short a little oasis for a poor, homeless person as I ran screaming to my mother but we don't know what's around the corner. We must walk in wisdom, being careful, looking ahead because the road we walk with God; if narrow, is under attack. Yet God has not given us a spirit of fear but of power, love and of a sound mind. *2 Timothy 1:7*

As Paul shares in the book of Corinthians "... we do not lose heart, even though our outward man is perishing, the inward man is being renewed day by day and our light affliction which is but for a moment, is working for us a far more exceeding and eternal weight of glory." Put another way, it is a really hard concept to believe this when we are in the middle of a trial but in the face of eternity our troubles are but a drop in the ocean and God has shown us that He cares about every detail. His grace is complete. Remember in Him we live and move and have our being. Keep in mind what God told me during the butterfly encounter? "Seek and you shall find." Well years after this experience, seeking has now become my life and in fact we are called by God to seek Him more deeply every day; in the same way, Jesus came to seek that which was lost. Many Christians will testify that when we step out to really fulfil God's purpose the Devil (our enemy) also steps out to block us. Being the master deceiver he will continue to come subtly and unexpectedly, catching us at every corner until we learn to fight and block him from our lives. Accordingly the road ahead becomes even more narrow.

Battle and Breastplate

Somewhere on that road the enemy came in and began to deceive and lie to me about my salvation. It is incredible to think that with my beautiful encounters with God and the wonders He has shared with me that such a thing could be possible but I began a season of terrible fear and utter despair. Just briefly, my daughter and I had attended a local church to try and find our feet following a house move. The preaching was unusual and a little disconcerting at times. It was not that the message was completely wrong just a little corrupted and I was really uncertain about staying there. However I attended an evening meeting and a discussion ensued about whether we could indeed lose our salvation. People seemed really excited about this teaching and keen to analyse the idea. I was very disturbed and decided to never return.   All our sins are forgiven and our salvation is reserved in heaven. The book of Peter, describes this as an inheritance uncorrupted and undefiled that does not fade away, reserved in heaven for us. It is not a doubtful salvation it is a blessed assurance. If it were not secure God's Word would be ineffective. 'He who hears My word and believes in Him who sent Me has everlasting life and shall not come into judgement but has <u>passed</u> from death into life.' If we have invited Jesus into our hearts and repented of our sins, we have already received eternal life and passed through death into eternal life, it has already been established. However a seed had been sown in my heart, just enough for the enemy to get hold of and start whispering lies to me. It was probably the darkest period of my journey with God. In essence God's Word teaches us that He works all things together for good and during this immense struggle and fearful period God strengthened my faith on many levels. The enemy assured me I had committed the unpardonable sin and had in fact blasphemed the Holy Spirit. I could actually hear audible words blaspheming and swearing at the Holy Spirit and I was propelled into deep darkness. However I never gave up and prayed deeply every day, every hour still worshipping Him and sharing my fears. An old friend assured me it was the enemy speaking and that I could not possibly blaspheme the Holy Spirit as I was already in Christ. It was a long and rocky journey and it took time to get through but I had two seemingly small incidents that began to reshape my walk and reinstate my position fully in the Kingdom. An act of pure faith because the terror was still there. Deep down I knew that it had to be an act of will to walk away from God and to reject His gift of salvation but my mind had been clouded and confused by the onslaught of the enemy. He will use any device he can to manipulate us and to turn us away from the truth. God's word says that nothing can snatch us out of Christ's hand and nothing can snatch us out of the Father's hand and there is no one higher than Almighty God.

How important it is to know these things, to know His Word, His Bible. If I had not had this grounding how could I stand? It is of the utmost importance. My first revelation came when God revealed to me the real truth about *Romans 8:9,* that I am *in* the Spirit actually inside the Spirit and nothing can take me out, my Spirit is in His. The second beautiful revelation came as I read a passage in Solomon. How it spoke to me, how I felt the love of Christ reaching me through those words:

"My beloved (Jesus) spoke and said to me:
Rise up my love, my fair one and come away.
For lo the winter is past the rain is over and gone.
The flowers appear on the earth the time of singing has come
And the voice of the turtledove is heard in our land.
The fig tree puts forth her green figs
And the vines with the tender grapes give a good smell.
Rise up my love, my fair one and come away."
Solomon 2: 10-13.

These beautiful, profound words sang to me and I began to glimpse an end of this dark season; hope shone on the horizon, but I had to come away myself, it was my decision. God highlighted this passage for *me,* it was speaking clearly to *me.* One day God showed me a line drawn under these fears it was a bright, shining line, underlining any frightening thoughts the enemy threw my way and any time subsequently I have had these thoughts, God has shown me that wonderful line. Another dividing line as He tells me "It is finished." Praise Him. Some day God may send me back to that church to breathe life into it and I pray that I will be brave enough to answer the call

So the devil attempts to ruin us but these attacks can have

the opposite effect and serve to strengthen our walk and our belief in God's word. It drives us to push in and find God like never before. The devil is never going to give up on us in the same way that God never will. We just have to learn to stand. The enemy is always attempting to knock us off the road but we can take small steps such as: trusting in Jesus, believing Him, recognising HIS authority, doing what His word tells us, submitting to His perfect will and staying fully armed.

Yet in all these things we are more than conquerors through Christ who loved us. Romans 8:37

"My brethren count it all joy when you fall into various trials knowing that the testing of your faith produces patience."

It is the testing of our faith, the testing that produces the fruit, not when things are going well but when they are bad or difficult or uncertain. "…but let patience have its perfect work that you may be perfect and complete lacking nothing." We need to persevere in our suffering and our day of trial because this perfects and establishes us.

Take up the whole armour of God that you may be able to withstand in the evil day and having done all to stand.
Stand therefore having girded your waist with truth having put on the breastplate of righteousness and having shod your feet with the preparation of the gospel of peace above all taking the shield of faith with which you are able to quench all the fiery darts of the wicked one and take the helmet of salvation and the sword of the spirit which is the word of God.
When you have done all to stand
And keep standing

We are to put on our breastplate of righteousness and *wear* Christ, we are sons of light, of the day. The armour takes the form of salvation, righteousness, faith, love, peace, truth, the Word of God and believing these things. Yet the armour is not submissive or passive it holds all the keys to victory but we *must* wear it. Paul tells us to put on Christ - to wear Him.

We may not be able to see that armour when we put it on. The enemy can see it though! The reflection of that armour is pure light and it burns!

When the Word says we are to seek first the kingdom of God, we begin to realise it actually *is* a kingdom with a King and His servants. Those servants are warriors clothed in humility. They must be equipped for the fight.

There is a parallel kingdom and its leader will never tire of fighting us and will never give up. But there is another side to the battle and that is of conquest. Going in to all the world; perhaps outside our backdoors or neighbourhoods and taking land for Him and bringing back what is His - the salvation of souls. ... by the armour of righteousness on the right hand and on the left.

My world at this time is outside my back door and I am trusting God to make me shine in a community where I am hardly known and as I pray and walk and take ground for the Lord I am trusting He will begin, right here, where I am. It is always worth remembering that our battle is not with people but with the devil. So when we take ground we know why there are strongholds. God's Word expressly states, "For our weapons are not carnal but mighty in God for pulling down strongholds, casting down arguments and every high thing that exalts itself against the knowledge of God." Amen. Halleluiah, there is always victory, as long as we *target* the enemy and *love* people. What a lesson that has been for me!

Remember we have, the Word, the power of the blood, the cross, the wonderful Holy Spirit to guide and lead us, our testimony, the full armour of Christ, the power to stand,

forgiveness. How can we lose?
The journey is the longest and greatest part of our walk, as is the climb in the building of trust. Many times now I find myself on my knees but there He is stretching out His hand to raise me up. He is the Great King! Arise shine for your light has *truly* come. When we find ourselves so sorry and so small, so uncertain we find His loving hand pulling us up out of the miry clay once more and onto the mountaintop where we can sing and dance waving our swords whilst He rejoices in our trusting Him.

In the Bible, Joshua was obedient and defeated his foes as did David, Moses and Gideon. Their power and weapons? Obedience to God and trusting fully in Him.

An incredible aspect of Gideon's victory, is his total lack of standing and status. A seemingly insignificant, ordinary man who took hold of the Lord's prophecy, believed it and became a great leader over thousands. Staggeringly Gideon turned to idolatry (worship of false gods) after fulfilling God's purpose but God still used Him and mollified his initial distrust with signs. Suddenly people followed Gideon and believed in him.

To further impact His Sovereignty God even *reduced* Gideon's army rather than extending it to prove that the battle was the Lords. God is really a transforming God whose light shone out from Gideon drawing the men of his community to suddenly follow this formerly lowly person.

As King David had proclaimed, "You are my lamp oh Lord, the Lord shall enlighten my darkness." for by You I can run against a troop, by my God I can leap over a wall." *2 Sam 22:30.*

King David himself was a reflection of faith and a true advocate of the armour of God. He was the embodiment of an exemplary warrior, a true inspiration. Through all his pain and suffering and sinful nature, he remained faithful to his purpose and to God, standing on the covenant promises. Even prophetically at a time of animal sacrifice, he looked ahead to forgiveness through repentance. He understood that God looks to the *heart* and was described by God as a man after His own heart. Way before Jesus had walked the earth, David communed with Him and walked in His Holy Spirit. He was a *faithful* warrior, a life constantly under attack, always on the run, suffering sickness and isolation yet still praising God and looking forward to deliverance. His life was hounded by others creating a real sense of adversity yet David translated this into bravery and into leadership over a band of outcasts and finally over Israel, as king.

As we step out and follow Jesus, our Shepherd we can draw a parallel with Gideon and David's men - stepping out to follow the 'one' we also follow the 'One' that carries the light and the truth. We *know* to follow Jesus, He says that if we receive Him we will know His voice and He will call us out by name and we will follow Him. Comparatively we *know* when others are gifted with Godly leadership, they carry something indefinable but we trust in it. "In His light we see light."

I asked God to reveal to me that indefinable quality that makes a genuine Godly leader and what made people follow them. He showed me it wasn't because of their character or their charisma, although this helps and often follows. It was because of an anointing, we cannot lead without it. If we are sincerely to lead people into the reality of Christ and the kingdom we need that anointing. David was anointed some time before He became a great leader and Gideon also experienced "the Spirit of the Lord coming upon him" before stepping out into battle.

There were times when David seemed to lose hope but he exchanged his fears for poetry and praise to the Almighty. He acknowledged that his enemies were too strong for him and he was overwhelmed, "He delivered me from my strong enemy, from those who hated me. For they were too strong for me but the Lord was my support." *2 Sam 22:17-18.* He gave God the glory, always. How mighty David was as he battled his enemies. As a young boy he was not fazed by the giant Goliath, instead fighting him 'in the name of the Lord' and finally taking his head off. *1 Sam 17:51*

It is another kind of battle at times, submitting to God's Lordship. Yet we hold on, hold on.

Eleventh Hour

I recall a film I once watched about King Arthur and Camelot. Rather than dealing with the usual exponents of magic and wizardry it had a very Godly thread to it. God was often referred to in a very biblical sense and light and dark were clearly defined rather than blending together, often supporting "in-betweenie" type characters. The film ended with a terrific battle between the evil Malagant and Lancelot. The fight combined swords, blood and physical stamina and to be frank it was really exciting. However I felt a little disturbed by this that the battle and its amazing choreography and passion should attract me so much. Was this God's best? The crescendo was pretty bloodthirsty but entailed the seeming victor (Malagant) standing triumphantly over the victim (Lancelot) just about to stab him through when Lancelot sees a flash of metal. Suddenly he has a second wind and finds King Arthur's sword lying nearby. Needless to say he grabs the sword and stands up, taking Malagant by surprise. He pushes him further and further backwards with Arthur's sword. There is great exhilaration and a sense of true victory as Lancelot manages to thrust Malagant's sword completely out of his hand and stab him to death, pushing him backwards into the throne that he so badly wanted to take from the king.

Similarly just when we have had enough and the enemy seems to be winning the battle, God will provide, Almighty Yehovah Yira will provide that sword of the Spirit and as we take it up we push the enemy backwards and defeat him once more. Suddenly you may find yourself unexpectedly rising up like the eagle and flashing your sword at the enemy, pushing him back. In a perfect walk we know exactly who we are in Christ. Standing on the mountaintop rejoicing. Here it is easier to take up that great sword. Somehow it is lighter and comes to hand more easily. It is almost effortless and uncomplicated. In darker times it is intensely heavy to lift up and sometimes we have to grapple for it; just like Lancelot and remember that we must depend on God completely and be willing to allow Him to grow us and to overcome - crucial to our walk. At length we begin to really know the different depths of battle and how powerful our simple words are. Never forgetting the shield of faith that quenches all the fiery darts of the wicked one.

Rise up and stand, take up the sword of the Spirit and fight with your mouth. Just as Jesus will fight the anti-Christ "with the breath of His mouth and the brightness of His coming." *2 Thess 2:8* His sword is His *very* breath and His light is so pure it will consume the enemy.

Transformation
Many years before the onset of my healing journey, I was lying in bed when God showed me a beautiful picture of a butterfly. The butterfly was trying to take off the ground; a bit like a great bird, but tied to its feet were large, numerous and very heavy bags. God showed me that butterfly was me. I was free because of Christ's redeeming work but I had too many burdens and could not be free to live my life.   God's ways are so prophetic because at the time I had no idea how much baggage I was carrying around. Can you imagine tying a tiny suitcase to a butterfly? Even if it was miniscule it could not fly with it.   Our healing in the Lord is both physical and emotional and these can be very intricately linked. Gradually over the years God has strengthened me and prepared me to face and deal with these things and has been steadily releasing me. I am not saying it is the end of the road but we are getting further on so that it is less and less about me and more and more about Him.   Just now before writing, Jesus took me on a little visual journey where I saw a beautiful white light. His hands were in the light and His face, joyful, smiling. Coming out of the light and flying up towards Him were many fluttering, white butterflies.   He clapped one of them in His hands as if to kill it to demonstrate His power can kill but He chooses not to. He chooses to preserve His children, because He loves us. He loves us so much that He died for us and He came to bring life not to take it.   As you can see butterflies have featured from time to time in my walk with Jesus! In my rebellious youth I searched continually to be happy and just

took freedom by the hand but it was the devil's hand and it really brought me into bondage, but praise God He did not leave me there. Placing HIS hand inside mine gave me the opportunity to take Him by the hand and let go of the world. A lovely, Christian friend once told me she saw me as a butterfly, that one day I would be free and just fly off. I believe that is Christ's message, 'you are free, in Me. ' Perhaps He also wants you to know there is freedom in Christ.

However, this freedom must come about by change. If we give our lives over to the King we will encounter a perpetual transformation. It is perhaps poignant to recognise that change can involve a great deal of pain but some will encounter deeper levels of restoration. Take courage, because His mighty redeeming power will continue the work. In time a deeper consciousness of His will surfaces necessitating our emergence from the chrysalis where we are birthed into the light by a loving, faithful Saviour. Never forgetting the pain of birth is always replaced by joy and always remembering: "He who began a good work in you will complete it."

He is My Son, today I have begotten Him.
He has now begotten us.

Jesus

As Jesus walked the earth He demonstrated much healing power dripping oil, myrrh and gold from His lips and fingers wherever He went. It appears that most of the healings were physical as He miraculously restored sight and ability to the lives of desperate individuals alongside curing leprosy and healing paralysed people. We can often focus on the physical healings of Jesus as Christians, sometimes forgetting that He also cast out demons and brought complete mental and emotional healing in His wake. The demonised man banished to the caves 'was restored and in his right mind.' after encountering the Great King. How incredible this must have been for such a tormented individual treated like an animal being isolated and chained. Yet Jesus released him causing him to leave this place of confinement and journey into town to testify of God's greatness.

When Jesus met the Samaritan woman at the well He understood her need for inner healing. He prophesied into her life and offered her living water. He did not judge her but prescribed that He Himself was eternal life along with the promise of the Holy Spirit. Jesus declares that whoever believes in Him, out of His mouth will flow rivers of living water. *John 7:38*

None of us can truly imagine that remarkable moment when Blind Bartimaeus cried out "Jesus, Son of David, have mercy on me." *Mark:46-47*. He knew who this Man was and could not hide his desperation. Who can really know the pain and torture Bartimaeus suffered? The inner turmoil and rejection. Yet he had faith.

Jesus responds by telling him it was is his faith that made him well. Long suffering has the impact of increasing and fuelling our faith. Interestingly the passage before this talks about greatness in serving. Bartimaeus could have been overlooked had the disciples continued to 'hush him' in the presence of the Lord. Do we need to keep our eyes open to what serving really is? Yet now for Bartimaeus - no more begging as he arose into new life given by the Servant Jesus.

Jesus in His mercy also forgave Zacchaeus restoring to him integrity and a valid place in his community. It is well know this short man's curiosity was such that he climbed a tree to get a look at Jesus. Or was he perhaps like Bartimaeus, consumed with faith and a desire to meet with His Lord to the same degree? Jesus knows all things and chooses the foolish things of the world and the unexpected. When He healed the woman with the issue of blood He became One with her; demonstrating again that it was her faith that made her well. The woman had carried this burden for twelve years and Jesus; after healing her, restores to life a twelve year old girl. Neither of them may have known that potentially as one was born and one began dying that Jesus would cross their paths simultaneously, and together through them glorify God.

So beneath the lines of scripture lies our emotional healing too. As our faith in Him goes from strength to strength; during trial, He has a habit of redirecting our steps and mindset. It's as though He finally manages to get our complete attention and draws us into deeper submission and ultimately deeper levels of relationship.

Our King was born to bring truth into the world and to save our *souls*. His healings were a demonstration of His greatness and divinity and a fulfilment of biblical prophecy; unlocking the mysteries of Isaiah 53.

Paul
Besides being the vehicle for a large chunk of the New Testament and the person to whom God chose to reveal many mysteries. Paul also reveals much about the background and inner truth of Judaism and Christ's corresponding role and position amongst His chosen people. He even reveals the deep, deep mystery of the inner sanctuary where Jesus established the salvation of our souls. He gives us a flavour

of grace enabling us to feast on the banquets of truth and salvation. Never losing sight of the price our Lord paid in providing such a gift for His children. Yet inadvertently he himself becomes a beautiful picture of healing and faith. He lives, breathes and acts out everything he preaches. The mysteries seem to come through much suffering. Through this suffering he derives an inconceivable measure of faith proclaiming and exhorting to the highest degree a Holy and faithful God.

The more Paul is pummelled and beaten and chained and destitute the more he gives glory to God. Our times of trial must maintain a focus. Even if in the midst of troubled times our concentration shifts; crossing over into fear, we somehow find ourselves re-focusing on His faithfulness - because He is Lord and moreso through times of difficulty.

Paul indicates that everything in this world is worthless counting it all rubbish compared to knowing God. He radiates a gift for transforming each trial into honour for the King.

How is it that our beatings really do refine us? Do they squeeze out of us all that is superfluous to glorifying Him? Only God can do this through us but he does it through people and circumstances, sickness and loss. True submission to Him seems to be about taking one step at a time as we recognise 'our times really are in His hands.'

Perhaps Paul's greatest attribute was in loving others more than himself. He promotes everything there is to promote about God's goodness and the work of Jesus recognising that in servanthood and lowliness we become like Him...the Great King that rode on a donkey and suffered more humiliation then we could ever know and all for us!

Paul states:

Your attitude should be the same as that of Jesus Christ.
Who being in very nature God, did not consider equality with
God something to be grasped, but made Himself nothing.

Taking the very nature of a servant, being made in human
likeness. And being found in appearance as a man He
humbled Himself and became obedient to death, even death
on a cross.

Recognising 'the giving' of the Philippians Paul honours
them by saying that he seeks what may be accredited to *their*
account rather than being concerned with the gift for himself.
Their eternal fruit not his. He breaks our hearts by declaring
he would rather be accursed himself for the sake of his
brethren. This depth of love can only be yearned for and
aspired to as we walk more closely with God. Paul managed
to stand before kings and governors just as Proverbs
promises 'our gift will make room for us' and reasoned with
the men in the temples. He desired that he might somehow
become *like* them yet without sinning; just like Jesus, to win
some for the kingdom. His character is designed to spill over
into our own hearts as Christ develops these attributes in us.
Yet deep down we know that to bear such fruit we must
submit and be willing to change. Suffering may sound
discouraging and it *is* whilst we are going through it, but if it
is in faith for a greater purpose it has the effect of crushing
us so that we may shine like Christ who fills the void.

Paul *knew* the scriptures he would have studied them all of
his life and so was able to relate and reason and to be taken
seriously. However he still needed God every step of the way
as he was frequently challenged and abused. Yet he kept
going..."and now compelled I am going to Jerusalem not
knowing what will happen to me there. I only know that in
every city the Holy Spirit warns me that prison and
hardships are facing me. Yet I consider my life worth nothing
to me if only I may finish the race and complete the task God
has given me; the task of testifying to God's grace. "
Acts 20: 22-24

There is a purpose to everything and a time. God's Word is
the same yesterday, today and forever. We run a race
fraught with similar challenges as Paul. These challenges
shape and prepare us for trickier races ahead. Without
challenge we remain babes, weak and soft with no concept of

perseverance or breakthrough. Without breakthrough there is no victory in Christ. He is the Head of the church, the Head of us. The Great Commander that we obey and follow after. He left signs of His coming along the way. The red chord hanging in Rahab's window was symbolic of His grace and death. Just like the red chord quickly tied to the hand of Perez as he broke through during childbirth. And so for Paul, Jesus breaks through unexpectedly and triumphantly on the Road to Damascus changing the destiny of a radical terrorist into the heart of Himself.

Jesus rose from the dead, taking the enemy by surprise, breaking the sting of death and making a way where there was no way.
Never forget He is the light in the darkness and He is shining through the cracks of His broken and chosen people.

My own life has not yet been perfected; it is still resonating Jesus' call up ahead. It has been greatly restored in terms of exchange; hatred for love, vanity for inner peace, brokenness for wholeness, fleeting happiness for pure joy and seeking His will over seeking fulfilment. I have travelled a long road with the great King and have learnt above all to trust Him. Even when things are really complex or we are holding on by a thread, He is our cornerstone. The Rock in the deep water and the Prince of Peace.

The night had been a deep struggle. Terror, torment, hope seemingly zapped. Sickness surrounded her very core. Death seemed to invite her, albeit undesired as she began to place on her armour; helmet of salvation, breastplate of righteousness. Somewhere in the distance she could hear audible words. Something about a crowd or a cloud, she couldn't make it out. She felt strength returning...waist girded with truth, shield of faith and embracing the treasured sword of the Spirit. Then she caught it "Great cloud, a cloud of witnesses. Since you are surrounded by so great a cloud of witnesses...let us run with endurance the race that is set before us." As Jess looked into the darkness of the night a picture began to emerge. A face lighting up the darkness. A smile so great, so huge it took her breath away. Somehow she knew that face and as she struggled to see it a picture simply formed before her and heaven came down. Now there are more smiling faces. They are clapping and cheering. To the side there is a finish line a beautiful white banner blowing in the breeze. Now she can hear them..."RUN they are shouting, RUN, don't give up, RUN!"

Hebrews 12:1

Mind of Christ

How can we know the mind of another? There is a secret place that God has placed within us - that of the mind. None of us can read the mind of another. We may grow so close to each other within our relationships and become very similar in action and deed. We may even have a hunch or a good idea about a person's thoughts or reactions. Yet none of us can actually know the thoughts of another person. What a gracious God we serve that He may give us a private space within, for our communion alone and for His. Take for example Vincent Van Gogh. A person seen to be stricken with mental health problems, an isolated, tortured individual. Yet none of us really know the true inner person. The one in the depths, the actual person within. Without doubt we can usually recognise a degree of mental health problem; that scripturally seems to be of a demonic nature at times. Those not in their right minds were healed in an instant with the Master's great deliverance. The One who came to set the captives free and we were *all* captive without Christ.

Yet Vincent was capable of producing works of genius. An ability to capture colour with an intensity and vividness hard to compare. The rough, beautiful strokes he used in his self portraits conveyed characteristics of sadness yet colourful genius hidden within the depths of the soul. His resplendent yet poignant sunflowers and the *dark* shine of the 'yellow house' both proclaim the beauty and creativity of a great talent. These inadvertently may reflect the depths of a wonderful Creator; albeit potentially unknown to Vincent.

So did this apparent tortured soul have a message to give? Unintentionally perhaps. Our critical world may see in pixilated forms or within closed brackets of time and understanding; somewhat masking the true character of a highly adept yet childlike painter. Which are both endearing and awe inspiring. We cannot argue that Vincent suffered trauma and distress within levels of pain that may be inconceivable for most. Reflected in the cutting off of his ear. The horrors of such self-mutilation do reflect a deeply anxious soul reinforcing the enigma of gifted genius perhaps separated from a loving God. One can only hope in the final moments of his suicide he called out and found Him.

So we have this secret place and we can choose how much we divulge, how much we share and with whom. It is a gift, a hidden sanctuary. A place for the storing up of wisdom and the thrashing out of pain. where we can commune with a Holy God. Who pouring in oil and wine restores the most broken of minds. We can then choose to share this secret place with a broken world pouring in oil and wine ourselves; bandaging the tormented minds and souls of others as we allow the Spirit and mind of Christ to flow through us to them.

Could it be when our gifts are not utilised for the glory of God or that we have little or no comprehension of the idea of a Creator that we have no sense of the purpose of our gifts? In a way imploding inwards to become a self-driven obsession. Something we are desperate to express which is unconsciously re-routed inwards. Or perhaps fuelling our desperation for recognition. I think most of us will taste this kind of phenomena. When Jesus takes centre stage breaking through the self-imposed empires of our minds we redirect these talents towards Him. He alone deserves the glory. Hard for our flesh but essential for the submitted soul and indicative of our walk towards the Light of Life rather than the darkness of self.

So we can have the mind of Christ. In the secret place where we can commune with Him alone where nobody else can enter that space. This is the secret place of the most high. Here we have allowed God to dwell within; where in His love He keeps us in check. Stilling our minds and correcting our faults - if we allow Him. The mind of Christ. The mind of Christ in *us*. The One who dwells in the kingdom that also dwells within us - those that receive His light and leading. The Bible tells us that the heart is deceitful above all things.

The heart and mind are closely linked. *As a man thinketh so is he.* The mind always wants to keep a little glory for itself so we must be careful to guard our hearts and minds; as we are taught to do. Yet with the mind of Christ within us He is changing us to be like Him as we learn to forgo our selfish desires and submit to His calling.

In the case of Vincent, did a little piece of God still filter through the cracks. Vincent who perhaps didn't know Jesus but still reflected that miracle of creativity. A beautiful gift. The gift that self imploded to become a persistent expression but ending in tragedy. Yet remains a captivating reminder of a God that gives of Himself.

Highway

There is a beautiful scripture in the Bible, "A highway shall be there and a road and it shall be called the Highway of Holiness." *Isaiah 35: 8.* I can rarely read this verse without crying. It simply amazes me that there is a holy road and a highway which is God's road, the road He has set before us. As we press in and seek His perfect will for our lives we will become more aware of that road. It may not be a physical road but it is the *journey*, the life of the disciple following after the King. Whatever stage we are on in our Christian walk, we are somewhere on that road. However the road is under attack. We cannot profess to knowing and loving God without the realisation of the adversary. There is an enemy of God and an enemy of people and that is the devil, that old serpent of old. When we give our lives to Jesus our awareness of the devil is raised because he steps up his attack against us. This should never be discouraging because our God is greater and His name is above every name. In the same way that God loves us with an everlasting, unconditional love, the enemy/Satan hates us with an everlasting vengeance. God's love for us is based on favour and grace through His Son, Jesus, whilst the enemy's view of us is based on an eternal bitterness and envy of the finished work of the cross and the Lamb's precious blood poured out for us.

"Jesus who loved us and washed us in His own blood!" *Revelation 1:5*

The power of the enemy is temptation, it is his only power because Jesus disarmed and defeated him at the cross removing his authority. Never underestimate the power of that temptation! He is 'the prince of the power of the air' transmitting a soundless and highly corrosive propaganda to barrage our thoughts and deposit seeds of destruction. Sometimes this can be so powerful it takes time to realise he is infiltrating our thought processes; sowing patterns of deceit that usually contain just enough truth to convince us we are useless or defeated or going nowhere. He wants us to give up. The key to our walk is recognising when he is speaking and then discerning the beautiful voice of our

Saviour. This takes time. Then being armed. However if we are not watchful that temptation can be extremely powerful and the enemy scarily subtle. Believing in Jesus also means we must acknowledge He became a curse for us; recognising a divine exchange where *all* authority has been given to Him in heaven and on earth. How wonderful that we too can walk in that authority and allow Jesus to fulfil His redemptive work in us and through us to others.

We are told to stand and resist temptation. Without Jesus this is futile because sin is veiled and it is just the natural way of the world. God has given us all a conscience as a safety mechanism but sin and darkness can seem like goodness and light before salvation. The world cannot perceive the wiles of the devil. Yet with Jesus and His precious Holy Spirit come discernment and a demarcation of the things of darkness and the things of light. That wonderful dividing line. When we turn to God our conscience is greatly enhanced, ever thriving for our protection. This seems to fit perfectly with the fear of God in order to help us respect His sovereignty and to stay away from harm.

...they shall be My people and I will be their God and I will give them one heart and one way that they may fear me forever for the good of them and their children after them. That I will not turn away from doing good but I will put My fear in their hearts so that they will not depart from Me. *Jeremiah: 32.38-40*

Sadly there are times when we close down our spiritual ears and do not resist temptation being drawn away by our own desires - just as described in the book of James. We can desire something so greatly that we may actually convince ourselves it is God's will for our lives. The trouble is it is the peace of God that rules in our hearts and when we choose our own way; contrary to God's best for us, we lose that peace and stumble about walking deeper into the darkness no longer hearing His voice at all.

I believe such a falling away only happens once on a big scale for a believer because the distance that accumulates between

God and ourselves is too hard to bear and we are driven back by His challenging, unchanging love. It is very true that when the enemy puts something in our pathway it will not be ugly or uninviting but it will seem beautiful and desirable; just like the fruit was to Eve or when a stranger entices a child into a car - they do it with sweets.

Remember "Be vigilant for your adversary the devil walks around like a prowling lion seeking whom he may devour." *1Peter 5:8*

Yet somehow we don't fall all the way because God is still there calling us up ahead. On that road, on the Highway. He calls us in our lack of peace.
Knock, knock.

 David illustrates this point in Psalm 35. He fell into sin attracted by the lure of beauty. "The steps of a good man are ordered by the Lord and He delights in his way, though he fall he shall not be utterly cast down."

God has a perfect will for us, to protect us and demonstrate His love through us. There is no doubt that who the Son sets free is free indeed but we have to remember what we are freed from "the law of sin and death." The enemy will do anything to get us away from that truth but Jesus will never let go. He promises nothing will ever snatch us out of His hand.

If we are not careful we can lose a grip on who we are in Christ. God has already told us in His word not to become 'unequally yoked with unbelievers' and there is good reason for that. When we start going in the wrong direction we have no peace and of course when we open the door to sin it all comes flooding in. This in itself exemplifies the direction we can take where God's work is slowly unravelled by temptation and the pull of worldly desires. Yet God in His mercy and wonderful grace has already forgiven us our wrongs and He has made plans for our lives. Apart from this He is far greater than the enemy or our own failings and I believe nothing will thwart His plans for long. It is worth noting that when Jesus sets us free from the *law* of sin and death, He also makes us free under the *law* of the Spirit of life. It is a law like gravity and will always work in our favour - the law of life.

There are some things that need to stay in the realm of regret, we must move on and do what we can *now* to make amends. Remember, pray, intercede. The mistakes we make have consequences and they certainly open our eyes but they can also help us to go deeper with God through realising when we are in the wrong. Bless His mighty name and His eternal forgiveness. The father was quick to place a ring and a covering on the prodigal son just like our own beautiful Father is quick to remember His covenant with us.

My own mistakes have helped me to truly love God with all I have to give Him because He died at a high price for me. I can never earn His love I already have it as a free gift. In Revelation, Jesus counsels us to 'buy of Him gold tried in the fire, that thou may be rich and white raiment that thou may be clothed.' Why do we need to buy? If salvation is a free gift why would we buy gold tried in the fire? It is because the buying is an 'exchange' He gave His life for ours, we take on His life and He takes on ours - destroying it in His blood and in the fire, as gold is refined. We take on Christ; His white garments and become like Him in this divine exchange, that we may become one in Him as He is One in the Father.

He truly loves us too much to allow us to do whatever we want. Just as we love our own children, so He cares for us. That wonderful submission and understanding of His grace tells me that whatever I do for Him must be motivated by love. If we truly love Jesus we will desire to please Him and surrendering wrong relationships and our sin brings us to a closeness with God we may never have dreamed possible. The greatest thing of all is there is always more of Him. If we *want* to go deeper.

I have sacrificed much of my life on many occasions and found this to be the catalyst to go deeper than I myself ever

dreamed.   This is when we   really find Him. For me,
something had changed within on the journey. If we are in
Christ, there is no fruit to keeping hold of ourselves.   In
reality we have died anyway!

Through sacrifice I rapidly began to experience many shifts in
my thinking, plans and desires.   I had in fact been all-
consumed with many worries and troubles that were building
great stumbling blocks on the road. I began to realise nothing
else in this life mattered as much as Him. He is everything,
our life, our love, our Shepherd, our direction and it is all for
His glory.   However the road remained tough.   Yet that is
God's promise to us, that in this world we will have
tribulation but fear not He has overcome the world.

Dear Reader

The pages of this book *do* reveal a journey. One that will always be in transition. Fresh challenges present themselves frequently and we are all on this journey together. If you know Christ that journey has a beautiful destination. If you do not yet know Him, please seek Him with all of your heart. He promises you will find Him. As Christians we often find ourselves navigating through the woods and craggy pathways once more. The deep climb of the soul nourishes the evolving landscape of a mind following Christ. A mind ever returning to Him, our faithful Shepherd. Oftentimes the rocky terrain beneath our feet does not reflect a more appealing landscape ahead which can remain fixed and stuck for so long. The tribulations we encounter seem to revisit us, reshaping into well-trodden paths presenting fresh challenges of previous trials. God will prevail. He is an ocean of faith to a weary mind and the water of life to a thirsty soul.

Hope

If there is one word Jesus has placed on my heart throughout these pictures and visions it has been hope. Our hope is in Jesus, our certainty. He *is* our hope, our light, our channel for peace. This hope is not the unsubstantial lukewarm hope the world knows but it carries an authenticity, the hallmark of a faithful God. His word assures us that, "hope does not disappoint because the love of God has been poured out in our hearts." Godly love cannot be forced, it is a fruit of walking with the King. When expressing this love to others we reinforce the element of hope, becoming a light in the darkness. These essential elements of love and hope can meet like the points of a diamond reflecting light back into a dying world; helping others to believe that goodness exists. Is this why God *commands* us to love? The Bible suggests it is His very essence. We too can mirror this intrinsic quality of Jesus, His very nature reproducing in us, without which, we cannot reach the lost. Love is a doorway into God's world. It offers a peek into eternity, shining a light on the prospect of something greater than ourselves. Loving others generates hope in their hearts, signposting them along the pathway of trust and relationship. This in turn may lead to salvation and in due course to inner healing and inevitable joy.

Power in the Blood
Remember, following our wonderful Jesus is so simple it's just submission to His majesty and Lordship.

However our passage through life and discipleship can take many twists and turns even though the road is the same.
We all encounter different struggles and mine has been a continual battle with sickness. However this has proved to be a refining tool of the Lord and a vehicle for finding His authority, through me.

Bee
It was now many years into my walk with the Lord, the healing journey had been long and God had been a constant source of encouragement. But could it be possible that God could use another insect to reach me? This time in the form of a bee? The mind boggles I know but God's ways are not

ours and He knows exactly how to reach each one of us in the heart in a way nobody else can. I have another powerful testimony to share and an opportunity to demonstrate that there really is power in the blood of Jesus. It is no mistake that the shed blood of Calvary has such significance. It was that critical sacrifice and the pouring out of His blood that not only washed our sins but overcame the enemy.

To Him who loved us and washed us from our sins in His own blood. Revelation 1:5

These are some of my journal entries throughout this time of healing,

18.07.10
Thank You Lord this day has been wonderful. Amongst the sickness and tiredness You continued to speak to me. You showed me the power of Your blood covenant. You gave me a real sense of the power demonstrated in Exodus, from the hyssop being dipped in the blood. I can see the weight of the hyssop, its bending backwards as it takes up the blood and the power it carries towards the doorpost. The strength it echoes as the blood is sent forth covering, sprinkling each post - securing the protection of those behind the doors. I felt a strength in the blood, a great authority and the power it had in protecting the children of Israel. You then brought me a personal experience of Your own shed blood and its power. The same type of blood connection but even more potent. You showed me how I am cleansed of my sins and forgiven. You sent a friend to visit - who I prayed would visit soon. I had been very down from feeling so unwell and my friend prayed with me and confirmed out of the blue that my sins were all forgiven. You knew I needed to hear this and that I had been wracked in condemnation all morning. Later in the day You led me to read Exodus and how Zipporah had thrown the circumcised skin of her son at Moses' feet. I see that she was confirming Your blood covenant to him. He was Your chosen vessel who would release Your people and perform Your promise. The skin was a reminder (thrown at his feet) that Your covenant never dies and was about to unfold. Also it was her son's foreskin, greatly symbolic of

Jesus, Your Son's covenant. Likewise in the most difficult of days You sent a friend to me. Did she come and throw Your covenant at my feet? A reminder that You keep Your promises and my sins are forgiven?

God showed me this deeper dimension of a difficult and seemingly random scripture that actually carries great significance and greatly empowered my faith in the blood and its continuation throughout scripture. Exodus 4:25

Pivotal to this continuation when Stephen was stoned, the witnesses laid their clothes at Saul's feet. God was carrying on that unchanging promise fulfilled from person to person; performing His wonders through man to fulfil His covenant. A spiritual baton transferred from Stephen and placed at Saul's feet. At a time when Saul was steeped in sin as we all once were.

Acts 7:58.

20.07.10

Yesterday there was a bee trapped in my bedroom. The window was open and the blind was shut. I opened the blind to give a way out for the bee but it could not find it. The window was open, there was an escape! I told the bee several times to go in Jesus' name but it did not or would not go. Knowing that we have dominion over creation I asked God why and what to do. Somehow I felt I was to observe the bee, attempting escape. The bee had one leg sticking out of the blind before I opened it and I saw the correlation between me and the bee with myself having one leg hanging out the side of the bed during days of sickness. I could still get up, there was still one leg hanging over. I wasn't completely confined just like the bee - there was a way out. The window was open but the bee just could not find it. You showed me another correlation that I was already healed but just could not find my healing. This was very powerful and it made me realise I was missing something. Each day I was trusting you and speaking out Your word over my sickness, which was all good and very effective but I was still missing something. Like the bee, I just could not see it. However I knew You would break through and show me Lord.

21.07.10

Tonight Lord I watched the Passion of the Christ with mum.

She was in tears and greatly affected but I felt different. I could feel Your pain and suffering but I also felt You were giving me an answer to something. I suddenly began to pray in tongues as Jesus was being beaten and whipped on the back. I became acutely aware that those whip marks really were for our sicknesses on such an inexplicably deep level, that I felt You *made* me watch this gory scene when I wanted to hide behind a pillow. Then you brought a revelation that it was the blood I was missing. The blood of Jesus was against this sickness. You had already healed me on the cross. I have always known this essential truth but I needed to acknowledge the blood and use it against the enemy. Thank you for the bee Lord. It was trapped in the window but only because it had not really seen.

Lord How could I it came as a deeper revelation amiss it? I do not know, only that I began to fight the illness with Your blood, coming against it every day until it eventually buckled under its power and bowed the knee causing my healing to utterly break through.

This period of sickness was and still is the best of times and the worst of times because although God never makes us sick He used this time to really reach me and truly demonstrate that His strength is made perfect in our weakness. If we are full of self how can we hear from Him? Being quite isolated and unwell for a very long time drew me to the source of everything. He really does work all things together for good in our lives. It was through this time of seeking and pressing in that His will for my life has been revealed. Ever faithful, ever true Jesus who has a purpose for each of us and calls us with a holy calling. He promises that those who diligently seek Him will be rewarded. His will remains, that we should seek Him with a pure heart and motive and desire to serve Him with the same. He is cultivating this in us, just as a farmer cultivates the land.

Help us Lord to trust You as You change us and establish us to be just like You.

Before God revealed to me the true power of His blood He

took me on a long journey of inner cleansing. Little by little He works in us what is good. He often works from the inside out and on my own path there were a great many stumbling blocks as God began to reveal; deep down I had become wracked with pain. All the hurts of my life had been stuffed inside but they could not be contained anymore because the merest sense of rejection or rebuff and I would go on an inner spiral of despair. I did not realise this as it was happening but I did know I could not stay in this place and God, of course was bringing me to freedom. This was not the fault of anyone else and I take full responsibility for my own misgivings. It was my own sense of failure and the deep roots of bitterness that were feeding a wilting, damaged plant. Suppression makes us fragile and over sensitive to others' decisions and is probably a root of rebellion. I wanted so much to forgive and God says we *must* forgive. Yet it was hard, every time I forgave, the same images or thoughts would rise up again and frequently I endured times of harsh, unforgiving thoughts toward others and myself. We do in fact have to forgive ourselves. This will provide our true healing. As we let go we come into agreement with God's will and agree that if Christ has forgiven us who are we not to.

Yet praise God He has healed that plant and helped restore broken relationships. His careful pruning and tending has been a painful process but I have welcomed it with great joy. I am so thankful now and on many levels have been a very happy, positive person but we cannot contain suppressed emotions forever they will always bubble up to the surface until we begin listening to the Holy Spirit. However inner healing may require a little patience, after all we accumulate layer upon layer - a lifetime of experience and growing that mould and shape us. This is in affect like the layers of an onion or the impressionable, hidden windows within. Sometimes the layers become like great, invisible walls to hide behind, shutting out people and pain, imprisoning the secret, hidden places that we choose not to reveal. Sometimes the walls become so thick that we have learnt to live within them and forget they are there. Fortunately God is in control as He slowly crushes the house and peels away the onion.

I had not realised it was the deepest roots of the onion that were penetrating and making me angry. Everything had become distorted and blown out of proportion:

With the enemy whispering in our ear and without knowing the proper tools of protection we can be misguided for a while. Remember God is always on the road, up ahead, calling.

Never fear it is just the journey and the Master Builder is rebuilding the walls. Paradoxically, it is a reality that the hidden, dark places of the heart actually hold the keys to the healing of our bodies, minds and souls. Jesus says we are to bring things out into the light where they can be dealt with, if they are hidden in the dark that is where they will remain. This does not mean we have to bare our souls to everyone shouting from the rooftops, but we must come clean with God and when appropriate with others. Healing always seems to follow repentance and part of the highway is that we do have to face ourselves and it is God who will take us through that transition. In the Psalms David frequently draws a correlation between ill health and sin and the importance of confessing our sins, "when I kept silent, my bones grew old," I said, "I will confess my transgressions to the Lord, and He forgave the iniquity of my sin." A single instance of confession and our sins are washed away. Just one drop of that powerful blood can cleanse the greatest of sins and refresh the darkest of minds. How wonderful God is how He will pardon us abundantly and heal those troubled areas.

There is a pure river of life, clear as crystal proceeding from the throne of God and of the Lamb (Jesus), in the middle of which is the tree of life and the leaves of the tree are for the healing of the nations. *Revelation: 22.* Once Jesus' blood has washed us clean, it will go on doing so, followed by that wonderful flow of living water as the Holy Spirit brings restoration to our souls. All we need is faith and the trust to allow Him in. God has healed me of so much and brought me on a journey of cleansing and forgiveness and at this time I can feel no trace anymore of pain or anger towards anyone. This really demonstrates how He is refining us moment by moment. How wonderful He is.

In this way, the Holy Spirit led me to a safe place where Christians were able to pray into these deep issues and set me free. His Holy Spirit penetrated places that were so walled over I did not remember them anymore but God did and He slowly released me. He also equipped me with the tools to protect myself; the full armour of God. Now I can link everything together, unforgiveness - the chief destroyer, rejection, sickness and demonic oppression from past occult involvement - even though it was experimental! I had let go of the occult the moment I found the truth but it did not want to let go of me and it was a real battle. There is always victory because Jesus has already fought that battle on the cross and the conquest of that amazing feat of time was now manifesting for me as I took up my own cross and followed Him. Preparing to let Him lead and shepherd me all the way to His great victory.

At the end of that healing journey He will take a great coring knife and grind out the depths of our souls piercing right through the inner layers of that onion - releasing the bondage and setting us free, halleluiah! It is a compelling notion that we must remain diligent especially following inner healing. "Be sober, be vigilant because your adversary the devil walks around like a roaring lion seeking whom he may devour. Resist him steadfast in the faith, knowing that the same sufferings are experienced by your brotherhood in the world." *1 Peter 5:8-9.*

Performance

Internal Fracture

Jess held her party glass, twinkling and shining like the pearliest teeth that glint. Her smile flashing like icicles, little glacier - bricks of invitation; a miasma of seductive platitude. She smiled again. Was it a winning smile or a steely cover hiding the fragile places within? Keep the pleasant exchange close to the panes, anything deeper may crack the glass. Staying alive entailed not wavering, not shrinking back. Get too close and those little glacier bricks will bite your fingers off. So she held her glass letting it sparkle and shine like the pearliest teeth that glint.

It is a major strategy of the devil to draw people together in a unity of isolation. Mask appearing before mask, a mirror image of the world's system which may inform a large part of our lives until Jesus comes in and we enter the slow but real passage of change. Masks and walls can easily gravitate into our Christian lives, but all the time we realise we are *being* changed there remains that wonderful hope. *"It is no longer I who live but Christ who lives in me and the life I now live, I live for Him"*

Jesus has dealt with all of our pain, sin and sorrow on the cross and as we receive our healing the work of the cross begins to unfold. We may not like facing ourselves but it is the only way, the tough squeezing walls of the narrow path, pressing out of us the dross to gradually reflect the shimmering gold of our loving Saviour. Nothing of self can remain, only self in Jesus, we live in Him and our walk on the Highway of Holiness is becoming ever free, ever closer to Him, ever more joyful. I know, I have walked it and am still there believing my Saviour and daily yielding more and more of myself to Him. When we submit and allow ourselves to be humbled by Him we actually become bigger and freer. The world dictates that we must be bold and tough and mask our real emotions because they are a sign of weakness and at best diminutive. When in fact the hardening only makes us smaller and less free as we become trapped within varying degrees of performance. In fact it becomes such a polished act even the actors are not aware of their role anymore as they seek to impress or identify or just to belong - fitting neatly into the world's expectations; a myriad of glass houses.

The world
So we can live in glass houses. Not transparent, open glass houses but fragile, easily broken houses prone to constant fragmentation, quickly crushed leaving sharp splinters. These fragments can be constantly mashed; pushed further inwards, out of sight into   deeper recesses of forgetting. When you live in a glass house the exterior of that house is everything.   It must be highly polished and beautifully reflective. The more reflective the outside, the more hidden the inside. These beautiful exterior windows have the power to dazzle their audience, taking the form of flashing smiles bringing the assurance of reciprocated admiration, the gel that holds the house together.   So fragile is this glasshouse that rebuke only hardens the exterior whilst constantly threatening the stability of the inner mashing.

Then Christ.
Now the glass house has been broken into; the shards of glass have been carefully removed, every last fleck of debris brought out into the light.   Now the glass is transparent reflecting *true* light, true colour, the colours of the King who dwells within.   On the outside of the house is a garment reflecting such bright light it is translucent but covers the house enriching its walls to bend and bow rather than chip and break.   That bright, white garment constantly buffs up the glasshouse as it rubs away the rough edges but it must be chosen and worn. A glasshouse *made* righteous reflecting the treasure within, sparkling, where even in the darkest of days the light can be found.

Within the Boats

A distinct lack of satisfaction seemed to prevail, causing her to keep treading the stairs of the upper decks, endeavouring to foster a greater sense of wellbeing and accomplishment. When falling overboard at various times she could simply climb back on board and resume the party even if in a slightly more injured vein. If seriously injured; perhaps by being stung by a particularly nasty jelly fish, she would seek out another pleasure boat. Unfortunately returning to lower decks of emptiness during the dark hours.

Without Jesus there is no light. Wherever we search the darkness prevails until we stumble across the lamp to our feet and the light to our path.

During a fearful storm in the Bible we find Jesus sleeping. He was fully rested and at peace when all around Him a storm was raging and shaking. He knew what was happening in His Spirit but He slept. He slept because He was fully immersed in the Father and His sovereignty. He trusted. Could it be that whatever boat we are on we can fully rest in Him? Could it be that when everything around us is sucking the life out of us and hardened roots are pushed to the surface of thin ground that we can remain still and at peace in Him? Could we still send roots deeper and deeper into Jesus as He feeds us life giving resource in the wilderness?

If we are fully submitted to the Sovereign Lord and actually sometimes when we're not, then every storm we encounter is from the Lord and every boat we find ourselves on is from Him. As a Social Worker I stepped onto a particular vessel believing it was a rescue boat. Instead it was tied at every corner by ropes that blocked any straightforward passage. It dragged through the muddy waters, catching on the wreckage beneath. Yet whilst on that boat, Jesus sent a tug to haul me to fresher streams. It came in the form of a Christian colleague who I could turn to and be refreshed with in the wilderness. In addition little sparks of light flickered as I picked small opportunities to witness under a tough anti - Christian framework.

In essence I chose that particular boat for myself which God honoured, but His will is sovereign in our lives and in time He plucked me off of that boat to heal and restore me to a place of greater submission. I now remained anchored in a boat of *His* choosing, a rowing boat where He was steadily increasing my strength to push forward, through the waiting period and into deeper waters of realisation and purpose. Patience. If we really trust Him we must not row ahead or lag behind but allow His breath to stir up the rivers of water around us and wait for His call to start rowing.

I believe God is bringing me to a place where I can row to the next boat, a fishing boat. A fishing boat has one aim and one purpose - to catch fish. It will sail through communities collecting souls for the kingdom. It is a boat that must face various storms and where its sailors must *themselves* throw in their nets. There is a lamp in that boat, bright, shining. Sometimes it reflects a mere shaft or a hazy shimmer indistinct but reflecting movement. No more than a chink perhaps or a lamp whose oil is running dry. No fear, there is an abundance of oil for that lamp especially whilst it is out to sea and fulfilling the great directive. When those fish are caught, they too, like their captors will be gutted and scraped clean. It will be the same Knife that lovingly cuts away the dross revealing more fresh wounds to heal. Somehow those fish will begin to sparkle echoing in their scales the loving Fisherman who actually *saved* them from the water causing them to die in order to truly live.

However it transpires before we can venture onto the fishing boat a period of preparation will commence. We must learn to steer the battleship first. The enemy will attempt to blow us off course as he assigns the powers of darkness to blind our way. We must travel through dark, shark infested waters and find out how to remain armed and prepared for battle. We become the conqueror that turns that battle around with our great shield of faith and swishing sword of the Spirit. This battle will then perpetuate onto the fishing boat where we become a boat within a boat within a boat. The fishing boat will have within its walls the dependable battleship that we have learned not to shake off but to hide within. The rowing boat will be safe within the battle ship as our inner man listens for His cue and direction. This is the deepest place, the secret place of our dwelling in the core of the boats, submerged in the blood of the lamb.

Before salvation, perspective is very different, my life seemed to drift along as I grappled for one raft after another. At some point these rafts bumped into a cruise liner, which could be termed the pleasure boat. I coasted along without direction, without purpose and enjoyed the party. At least I enjoyed the party on the upper decks. The lower decks provided times of loneliness and fear.

In His perfect timing Jesus introduced me to a different boat, a lifeboat where I felt safe and mingled with a different kind of passenger.

Yet unwittingly I have jumped onto another kind of pleasure boat at varying intervals and am still capable of this without giving Jesus pre-eminence and proper Lordship. We have all been given an *essential* vessel provided to take us through life and to enable us to live on earth. How wonderful it would be to glide in that boat through still, soft waters. Just like those 1950s pictures of cruise liners with everybody smiling. It is a possibility but life teaches us that the journey isn't soft but hard and sometimes glides but also collides with unexpected storms.

He must rule and reign, He knows what is best.

A disciple is essentially a disciplined one. For Christians it seems this is a hard concept. It certainly proves a struggle as we steadfastly focus on developing our relationship with God and transforming our souls yet fail to look after the wonderful machine God has given us to function in. I believe many of us struggle with this and we must take action before we become trapped on another pleasure boat and no longer have the strength to row to the fishing boat; let alone our preparatory battleship. Oh how the enemy smiles as we wilt in unhealthy lifestyles and drift out to sea, marooned in our weak and lethargic dinghies, failing to ignite our passions to serve the Lord. The enemy is subtle and crafty and we must be watchful of his wiles in every sphere of life. Bringing our will in line with the true Master, Jesus will place a seed of counterattack in our spirit and kick the enemy off of our boats. It will be a battle seed, a righteous anger at the enemy and just enough disappointment in oneself to want to take the step of overcoming this wasteful aspect of life. Praise Him.

He is now Lord of the ship. How important this becomes and how gracious He is as He slowly works in us what is good, little by little.

In John's Gospel, people looking for Jesus were so determined they were willing to get into boats and seek Him out. How blessed we are in one sense that we only have to journey within ourselves now; to the kingdom, to find Jesus, but how wonderful to actually get into a boat and go and search for Him. When they find Him Jesus surprises us by acknowledging that they were only seeking him because they had been filled. He reiterates that He is the bread of life and that we will never hunger or thirst on knowing Him. We are to seek *Him,* the bread of life, leading to everlasting life.

Times of refreshing always come when we walk across the waters of life and towards Jesus' own boat. Here He meets us just where we are. There may be a storm around Him but He will reflect calm and tranquility. There may be darkness but there will be a light around Him as he smiles and reassures. Even if He disciplines He will bring about that quiet hope. Can you see Him in the boat? He may seem far away at times; so deep in the waters, but if we press in we will find Him.

Yet even if we have lost all sight of where we are going Jesus will provide a raft or a log to hold onto until we conquer battles of confusion, lost in the wilderness or marooned out to sea with just His name to guide us:

"Jesus," "Jesus."

Jess dived in, initiating a sharp, definitive crack in the deep, deep waters. Then wading through His Spirit - filled words, immersed, complete, she swam back to shore; stones rolling backwards, creating a little fizzing sound as she left the richness of the water. She couldn't resist looking back, just once more, a final glimpse. Now climbing the rocks, the hills, now a mountain she looked up to see her King once more; in His hands a rope. He let it down. "Come." He said. Safely and securely the rope was now in her hands as she climbed the mountain to meet Him. On the other side He placed His hand on her back as she climbed the steepest hill. She was struggling but He was there by her side. Now at the top she found herself running down, with a hop and a skip she leapt headlong into the grassy valley. Soft, verdant the valley was a welcome spring in a dry, dusty land. Her feet like the feet of King David, like a deer trusting in each dependable step. Here in the lush valley gentle rain fell barely touching her as it sparkled and shone in the dusty sunlight.

Times of refreshing

Water

He who believes in Me, as the scripture has also said, out of
His heart will flow rivers of living water.
John 7. 38-39.
The Sanctuary

There is a place inside us, a deep well of longing.
It sits and tugs and reminds and pulls yearning for
completion.
An abundant, unfathomable desire, pulling us ever closer to
the source of life.
In this abundance comes a pouring out of holy rain, His Spirit,
softly falling, as it forms into a sceptre of righteousness in
your hand, into a golden bowl, outstretched, wide open.
Waiting to be ever filled with You oh God, our Father, our Lord,
our all sufficiency.
An absolute immersion in the water, in the life of Christ.
The anchor of hope, of eternity, of indwelling, never letting go.

"Therefore with joy you will draw water from the wells of
salvation."

Flow

Stand on the beach and just witness the pull of the tide.
Although it is linked to the moon's gravitational force it is
still God's grand design. Close your eyes, feel the ebb and
flow of the sea. The mighty power of God, His breath in
motion with yours, every ebb, every flow, feel the power as He
draws you by His Spirit to commune with Him at the rising of
the sun, at its setting. Every morning every night, breathing
with Him as He comes round again, like the sun, like the
tide.

In the sea is a boat, where Jesus sits. He is waiting for you
and for me. We need to get into the boat and get out to sea
but we cannot get in until we fully trust Him and not
ourselves. As the tide of the sea pulls in and out with such
power and such momentum so we must breathe with God, in

and out.
"Breathe in My Spirit that is the life."

Proverbs speaks of wisdom as a flowing brook. There is a connection between wisdom and this type of water. Picturing a brook, the bubbling upwards of the fresh water, constancy, peace, serenity, unchanging, clean, fresh - the well of wisdom. The Holy Spirit in ourselves, the water, bubbling upwards coming up and out of our mouths as He passes through the heart, purifying, cleansing - the well of wisdom.
I see Lord, that living water.

The essence of that water has power and might as well as being gentle and calm. Scripture is a treasure chest of these qualities. 'As the deer pants for the water brooks (His wisdom), so pants my soul for You. ' 'Deep calls unto deep at the noise of Your waterfalls. All Your waves and billows have gone over me,' …'a pure river of water of life, clear as crystal proceeding from the throne of God and from the lamb.' The power and majesty of those constant waves and billows refining, cleansing.
 There are times when the waves are flowing back and forth in tune with the
King but oftentimes we have to wait on the Lord. It may be that we need to adjust some particular line of thinking, perhaps a wave of unforgiveness or a self centred act. Our spirits know when we are on track when we are following the Shepherd. The peace of God will be there, we will dwell in His rest. Yet sometimes we must brave the waves, just knowing He is there because He promises He will be. If we fall He will put out His hand just as He did to Peter. It is in the waiting that our trust is put back together; correctly assembled again, taking on clearer proportions and deeper waters as our hope begins to bubble up to the surface, bobbing on the depths of His love. His creative, restoring water, ever filling, ever seeking out.
You lead us beside the still waters Lord and there restore our souls. You are the fountain of living water and that water has been given to us to pour into the lives of others, allowing Your Spirit to seek out and fill that which was lost. Water seeks out and finds every corner and leaves no part untouched, every

crevice, every crack until it is all filled, all washed.

Deep calls unto deep.

In the same way there is inexplicable depth to the cross. Deeper and deeper levels going inwards and stretching out North South East and West, no beginning and no end. Jesus has inscribed us on the palms of His hands. He inscribed us with His blood and the nails. His feet turned inwards on the cross so that we would always turn towards Him and follow. His arms outstretched so that we would embrace all those He embraced, with love and compassion. So we must stretch out our arms and bear all, declaring everything He did for the world. His head hung low in submission to the Father. That beautiful crown of thorns a divine exchange, His blood for our crown. Trust in Him for He is faithful and it is finished.

Jesus is the way the truth and the life but He also says: "Where I go you know and the way you know." We need to be rooted and grounded in Him, rooted in His truths where He will never let us go. The wind and storms around a plant make its roots push deeper in to the ground just as we must push down deeper into the King into the truth, into His Word, to know His way.

Where can I go from Your Spirit Lord?

I am in the desert and the wilderness
In the deepest darkness, in the brightest light
I will never leave you, nor forsake you

Who are you rooted in? You are rooted in Me?
Turn and run my roots will seek you out and draw you back.
Hide in a cave and my roots will find you and bring light to
guide you out.
I am the way the truth and the life
The Tree of Life

Tree

Walking back from a long journey into town; the sun beating down and her mouth dry from the parched air, Jess sought the Lord. Almost the entire journey had been spent in earnest, inward prayer, desperate for His deep, satiating presence. She worshipped, she called, her heart beating, dehydrated but resonating a hollow, persistent drum - roll. I am the King, the Tree of Life bringing glimpses of a future I prepared long ago; droplets of water to a thirsty soul and glints of a purpose that powerfully crush flickers of doubt. How she loved Him.

Walking the dry path she suddenly became aware of an awesome pine tree. To the left of the path it stood, towering. She was awestruck by its beauty, its majesty. She heard the powerful, inward call of the King. "I am the tree of life, it is My majesty you are feeling, My presence. Whoever eats from this tree will live forever. I am the tree of life, I am in the midst of My Father's kingdom. My roots are in Him. Come to the rivers of life that feed that tree. As I am within you, those rivers of life will flow through you but the roots are in the Father. The kingdom of God is within you so feed on those roots, let Me nourish you."

Jess began to draw near; feeling the damp coolness under the welcome shadow of this great tree. She began to consider the benefits of such a tree on this hot, sun filled day. It shelters from the heat, giving shade and rest. Under its shadow is a peace and a rest, inviting one to sit and be still to recover from one's journey. It has depth and colour. Its branches and pine needles are dark and convoluted, striking a desire to look deep within it and unfold its mystery. She considered Jesus as this great tree, statuesque. The open branches as outstretched arms and open hands gathering His children to Him, as a man gathers wood for the fire. Carefully selecting His children, the ones that will love Him and enter into His grace; who laying aside fruitless notions of self righteousness are clothed in *His* light in *His* robes of majesty. Under that tree children can play, safe from harm. They may wander freely within the boundaries set out by a loving Father. They may wander too far and God may allow that but He is always looking down to the one under the tree and the one afar off. Tending His children and drawing them close, under and into His shadow.

The tree of life gives oxygen - that is His breath and His Spirit. We could envision Jesus as the tree of life in the Garden of Eden, then hanging on a dead tree in Golgotha only to become that living tree in heaven. Jesus is also the Word, the Word of God that cannot be separated from who He is. We eat from the Word, from the tree. He sustains us with His words and the truth of who He is, who we are and who we will become; in the end like Him.

Feel the roots pulling you back like the ebb and flow of the sea. Like the pull of reigns as we allow ourselves to *be* rooted and grounded in Him. In parallel we are to abide in Him. Jesus says He is the true vine and the Father is the vinedresser.   He is the vine and we are the branches. Subsequently the branches cannot bear fruit of themselves. We have to abide, experience the tree of life, feed off of Him and receive His life giving power. Jesus promises that if we abide in Him we will bear much fruit and that we shall be His disciples. Sometimes it really seems that we are not growing much, perhaps not bearing fruit but if we look over the healing transitions and life challenges we have come through we witness the fruit in ourselves. Perhaps we no longer feel comfortable swearing or over eating. It may be that we share our witness of God with greater love and compassion, perhaps we _can_ love now. God in His kindness continues to prune us that we may abide and continue abiding.

God promises us that if we trust in Him, He will provide all of our needs and He will save us even though He gives us the

bread of adversity and the water of affliction. His healing rivers smooth out the rough places as we trust.   If we delight in Him He will give us the desires of our hearts. We shall be like a tree planted by the rivers of water just as

Jesus is planted in the Father and puts forth the rivers of living water, we will bring forth fruit in its season and our leaf shall not wither and whatever we do shall prosper.

As we abide in our home He will abide with us where we can be one in Him and the Father. We will never be thirsty because His rivers will quench every appetite for Him and our leaves will be green and abundant, perhaps they will be for the healing of the nations as we step out, take risks and believe.

Ps 1.3. Ps 37.4. Isaiah 30.20-22

A Moment of Encouragement.

Banqueting Table
I was given a picture of Jesus in a pasture, as Shepherd. He was looking for and calling His sheep. He was calling them home to Israel, perhaps the new Jerusalem. He placed a bag of money in my hands to demonstrate he gives abundantly and that He provides. I then saw an incredibly long table leading through the pasture and up over the hills, it was intentionally long. He wants me to earn my keep in the kingdom to become a labourer. To bring the one and the ones to His table set for the millions. I saw many Christians doing their part, some bringing one or two and some many to the table. As each one of us does our little bit we are filling the table for the great supper. The table is long, set four square and one day we will eat with Him and see the fruits of our labour.

Highest Aspiration
Slowly, slowly then as we walk with the King of Kings and Lord of Lords the grafting in of the kingdom takes on greater dimensions and depths until an undetectable fusion occurs.

The dissemination of our pain wielding its way back to the cross effects a propagation as we begin to flourish and spread out like a native green tree. Our roots and branches become more powerful as they are tightly clipped and bear incredible fruit through the all encompassing pain of transformation. So we are changed bearing this abundance of prolific fruit that rings sharply of Jesus and glorifies Him. Our former condition now fading as our hearts and minds become entwined and knitted together with the King. Always gravitating towards Him. 'Christ in us the hope of glory.' Oh Lord change us to be like You. Prepare us with a determined, unyielding resolution to tread the path set before us and fulfil all Your purposes in us. May we recognise this life as transient; keeping our eyes fixed on You, magnetised by Your awe inspiring, mind blowing faithfulness. Your creativity in preserving our uniqueness whilst modelling our unity as one.

Help us Lord to be all that you made us to be, may we reflect
all that you died for and embrace the summer ahead.
For lo, the winter has past.

Jess entered the garden. Looking intently she saw a shrub forming into a great oak tree and a fine-looking rose bush abundant with life. He was there, He showed her His hands they were dirty from digging deep within the ground. The soiled, hardworking hands of a keen gardener. "You have worked hard for me!" She exclaimed. He smiled. Lord you have dug out the rubbish, the worms, the beetles, the maggots and produced a beautiful rose bush - perfectly neat with a little fence encircling the beautifully tilled soil. It was a gift, a gift of love. Then she realised it was her, the rose bush was her! Gradually a tree came into view, the great oak. It's trunk gnarled and strong, it's branches many and its leaves almost raining in abundance of deep green like the best oil or the rarest of stones. She knew there was more work to do and the rose bush and oak were glimpses of who she would become. Suddenly she was sliding down under the soil, deep, deep. She saw the deepest part of her 'a root of bitterness' she knew He would pluck it out and that she would begin to flourish. As she rose above the soil He wrapped around her a white cloak and on her head He placed a crown.

Vision
&
Love of the Father

Pictures from the King

Sometimes we know that we know that God has promised us something or told us something. It is revealed to us in the truest part of us within the heart, in the depths.

Our journey with Jesus is like being on a starting block. Oftentimes we run too early or too late. Sometimes we want to run but cannot run at all. Then we start off well and we stumble and then again and stumble further. Then we hear His voice maybe a faint whisper but we know when it is Him. He might say "Here I am or come seek and Me." He may just express His love or show us where we are going wrong. "Come, start again - trust Me, follow Me, ask Me." Then we find ourselves praising Him again and everything starts to fit together once more. The wonder of God is that we can start over and over and over again.

"One thing I do forgetting what is behind and reaching forward to those things which are ahead. I press toward the goal for the prize of the upward call of God in Christ Jesus." Philippians 3: 13-14

Submission

At some point on my walk I desired to go deeper than ever before with God. At this point I had walked with Jesus for around ten years, loving Him and giving my life to Him. Yet I was missing something very vital. My life had changed the instant I met Jesus all those years ago sat in my friend's armchair. Yet now it was rapidly changing.

I was finding that the more one submits to Him, the more everything makes sense - it all begins to fall into place. The book of Proverbs says we are to "Trust in the Lord with all our heart and lean not on our own understanding. In all our ways to acknowledge Him and He will direct our paths." *He* will direct, *He* will lead. We do not know how we are getting there but He will take us. It is the ultimate trust, walking on water. "The steps of a righteous man are ordered by the Lord so how can a man know His way?" Never forgetting that this righteousness is from Him, we are *made* righteous.

So I began to really trust as never before and to open my

heart even to the depths. I began to seek *His* will for my life. How simple that may seem to some but how easy it is to miss it. I began to realise that I was living my life by my own strength and not His, but how gracious He is. It is Him who is working in us anyway and changing us into His glory and this is a process of time but we must submit to it and I believe, really desire it. God never pushes His way into anything. Now I was beginning to live my life for Him and to seek *His* will, and how quickly my life began to change. It was a speedy transition. A quickening of the heart to follow Him and a paling away of everything else. I spoke this prayer over my life and it changed everything:

Lord pour Your will, Your dreams, Your vision, Your purpose, Your plan, my destiny, Your desires into my heart. Pour them in Lord like a fountain and make them happen. That I may do and live out my life in You. That these things become my dreams, my vision, my purpose, my plan, my destiny - in You, through You and for You. Amen.

The things of God are spiritually discerned, that's the whole point - He is Spirit and our spirits connect with His, eternally. These things are not always logical or within our own understanding but we know when it is Him and when He is reaching us.

It was a while before I could understand what was happening to me. I now know, subsequent to the prayer I prayed, the experiences I had started with a burden from Him, but never having experienced anything quite like this it was difficult at first to comprehend. I began to have a growing and deep compassion for the lost and hurting people of the world. I felt that I was carrying something in my heart, so much so that it drove me to press in and pray constantly. I had a sense of something about to happen or to be revealed. I prayed continually and felt deep impressions of things the Holy Spirit was showing me but in the beginning could barely catch them. I know there was a shift away from myself and into the things of Him. This was the place I had been aiming for and it is true we must bring our cross daily to Him and recognise what He has done and His Lordship.

These *journal entries* go back to when I first began submitting to His will. Much of it is addressed to Him because it is a pattern of prayer and vision and He is the person I communicated with throughout. This is the journey of His will unfolding and the journey of answered prayer.

July 2009
Lord I cannot quite remember the sequence of events and things you have shown me. I do know that I began to pray into your will daily. This with the act of self sacrifice has become a fire within. An inner joy that seems to be superseding the difficulties of life has become a guiding light. I pray Lord that I have set my hand to the plough and set my face as a flint - against all odds, faith.

During this time I began to have severe attacks from the enemy; he does not like it when we step out in faith.
I began to have dreams that were visited by You.

Dream 1
I was standing on a precipice. A tiny triangular corner on a high building like a tower. There was no way off. The precipice was as big as my feet and I fit right into it, there was nowhere to go. I considered climbing upwards and looked up over my shoulder. The building was a great height and I did not think I could make it. Suddenly I heard Your voice say, "Trust Me!" I knew it was You and immediately I jumped from this great height and landed securely on a white step. As I landed I knew it was right, it was perfect, square. Immediately after this I went in to a hall like a community centre and began to evangelise and witness to people about You.
End of dream 1.

Prior to this I had a long period of indecision. I had still been unwell for a long time and had returned to work at one point and had to leave again because the illness was so chronic. I had been praying amongst other things whether to leave my job and continue pursuing God's will. I really could not decide because the income was so needed and the thought of leaving the profession I had worked hard for was very tricky. Yet I knew I was not fit enough at this time and had not yet received my healing but was actually getting worse. I felt the stress of my job was adding to the sickness. Like everyone I have had many dreams but I can isolate these four dreams, knowing they were from God. When I awoke from the first dream I knew without any doubt it was from Him It was so plain and I felt it was some sort of answer but I did not completely understand it yet. However, clearly, God wanted me to trust Him.

Dream 2
The second dream was extremely profound. I was walking through a well-known town to myself, when I was suddenly going through a tunnel that entered into heaven. The tunnel was light and white but still on earth and in the town. As I approached the end to enter heaven I passed by some Christian friends who were welcoming me and playing instruments. They were all dressed in white and whilst there was a sense of curiosity from myself there was great joy and celebration from others. As I approached the end further, I looked ahead and there was an oven. People were being thrown into the oven, those that had not received Jesus. I knew I would not enter heaven yet because I had to tell people, had to bring the love of the gospel and bring salvation to lives.
End of dream 2.

Again on waking I knew this dream was from God. Although God has already told us as Christians to go into all the world and share the good news, I felt this was further confirmation of something God had in mind for me personally. I pressed in and kept praying.

Dream 3
I was in a very small church meeting. I stood up and felt filled with the Holy Spirit, challenged, very nervous but really bold. There was a newness in me. I literally felt the Holy Spirit like a fizzing in my hands in the dream. I went out into a community centre and started laying hands on people and

telling them about Jesus. Many people were prayed for and I believe came to salvation. I held hands with someone in a wheelchair and he got up and walked.

Oh that these things might become reality Lord?

End of dream 3

Dream 4

I dreamt I was on a high place, a fort in a very significant place. I was very high up and trying to climb up passages and steep banks. Someone was behind me doing the same thing. I climbed a very steep bank and then realised I was stuck. I called to the person behind me for help and he reluctantly brought me a table from somewhere! However just as he did this I reached the bottom then continued climbing through banks and passages. Suddenly it became very cold and icy and I had nothing to hold onto. At one side of the bank was a sheer drop - it was masked by darkness as of night time and thick fog. I could see a lit square cut in the bank to one side. Although it was high up I could reach it and climbed over to it. I looked behind me at the sheer drop and suddenly knew I was in a dream and that God wanted me to trust Him and fall in to this great abyss. The unknown, where he would save me and show me where to go. Even though I knew it was a dream and that He would save me I lost courage and reached towards the square where I somehow lifted myself up and continued on.

End of dream 4.

At this time I was still in a place of indecision about my job and other issues and believed this was a part of the trusting process. I did eventually give up my job and it was definitely becoming too heavy a load. God showed me in this dream that He is in control but even if I wasn't ready to trust fully He had a way out for me - through the square. Also a few days before this God gave me a word.

Word from the lord.

I am waiting for you to put your trust in Me completely. Keep reaching, climbing. As you climb to Me I will reach down My hand and lift you up.

I began to have odd visions of myself bending down and getting things out of cupboards. I would be in my kitchen and suddenly have a flash or picture of myself getting food out of cupboards for others. I seem to be a leader. I have no idea why this is happening but it goes on for some time. I begin to understand that I will be involved in something. Lord You showed me rain pouring over me as prophetic words, I believe there is more rain to come. Sometime later I sent for a prayer cloth from an evangelist which I felt led to do. When I opened the letter from him I felt the power of God go through my hands. The prophecies He sent me matched almost identically to those I had written down and was praying over my life. At length there became a daily knowing in my heart and a new kind of authority. I asked for a sign that was confirmed. I also felt led to buy two books at perfectly synchronised times that helped my walk enormously.

I began to ask God what this burden was. I received words from Him from the Bible which I wrote down:

I will never leave you nor forsake you.

I have anointed you to preach good tidings to the poor.

Enlarge the place of your tent and let them stretch out the curtains of your dwelling. Isaiah 54:2.
Unless the Lord builds the house He labours in vain who builds it. He is our sure foundation. The rock and anchor of our hearts and hope. Praise Him.

Trust in the Lord with all your heart and lean not on your own understanding. In all your ways acknowledge Him and He shall direct your paths. Proverbs 3:4-5

Commit your way to the Lord trust also in Him and He shall bring it to pass. Delight yourself in the Lord and He shall give you the desires of your heart. Ps 37:4-5 I believe this truly means that it's not our own desires but that He places the desires within us - He gives them to us so that His desires become ours.

89

A man's gift makes room for him. Prov.18:16

The kingdom of heaven is like a mustard seed which a man took and sowed in his field. Which indeed is the least of all seeds but when it is grown it becomes a tree so that the birds of the air come and nest in its branches. Matt 13: 31-32.

Torchlight Vision
Why was God giving me these verses? Why was I carrying this burden, these thoughts and pictures? I sat on my bed one morning and asked God to show me.

A picture formed before me and it was as though God literally played a film before me in the air....
I now understand this to be an open vision.

Lord I see two mountains equal in size, one is a bit further behind the other. They are not obstacles but great dreams to be climbed and conquered, in that I will dance between the two; the nearest first. In fact I will jump between the two. Now I see snow on the first mountain with a light above it. The light is beginning to shine through a cloud within which are hands. There is money raining down from the hands into a basket on the top of the mountain. The further mountain is now coming into view with snow on top and both mountains have clear, clean water like ice trickling down the sides of the mountains. Straight, neatly in four lines. I believe they are facing North, South, East and West.

There is now grass growing on the mountains and sheep and goats are feeding there. There are flowers and springtime. Now there is rain coming down on the first mountain. The money remains dry and shining with just one or two drops of rain on it. Now I see the green prayer cloth. Whatever this vision is Lord You are going to fund it. I see the prayer cloth being rung out and dripped into the basket, but it is shining. I see Jesus beckoning me from the other mountain. There are wolves around the mountain, He is keeping them at bay. He is the Shepherd. He is pushing me towards the wolves but pulling me back as though he wants me to conquer them through Him. I see liquid myrrh and gold in abundance. A castle of protection.

A few days later God revealed to me the vision:

Following my prayer request the night before Lord you woke me early hours of the morning and explained to me the vision. You asked me to set up a charity or community place (just as Your dreams showed me) within a specific geographical area. Praise You for answering my prayers. You said you wanted to reach the people of this area. You asked me to pray for someone and that day the prayers were answered. I believe the prayers were to be a confirmation that it was indeed You speaking to me. The first mountain represented a charity the second mountain represented evangelism. I had been feeling a leading desire to evangelise which really reflected the second mountain of the vision. I believe there will be a merging together of these two important vehicles to reach people. The four lines of water have a global emphasis that I now know to be Israel. Praise You Lord! Thank You.

A very profound witness for me happened a little while after this. One morning before I left for church; during prayer God told me I would reap one hundred fold in His kingdom. I prayed for a confirmation from the Pastor. During that service the pastor spoke to many people from the front. His words to me were that I had the potential to reach tens, hundreds, literally thousands of people for Christ. I knew he was going to speak to me just beforehand, through the power of Almighty God. Thank You Lord for this confirmation and Your faithfulness. I have since had a word from another Christian that I would reach thousands for the kingdom. All glory to God, His will be done.

Amongst many other verses, pictures and little things You are showing me Lord. You asked me to draw a picture of a lit torch and run with it. I perceived this was to call the charity Torchlight and I drew the picture. At the same time I was reading one of the books You led me to read. I turned to a section about ancient Greece. At the time of the Olympics there was a torch race which had no bearing on speed or fitness but whether the person's torch was still burning when they hit the finish line. You have put that burning torch within me and I pray You will keep it stoked up until I finish the race. As I understood this I opened my Bible to look up a verse but instead found an account of evangelism speaking of it as a burning fire - another witness?

In these early days of revelation about the ministry I suffered much frustration because I had not as yet received my healing and was quite house bound a lot of the time.

10.07.10
I see a house, I have a torch in my hand given to me by the Lord. I am not designed to just walk about the house with the torch but up the pathway and up the mountainside, but the house is a beginning, a place for prayer, a starting point. I am like a stag right now my feet are stationary but pacing the floor as if ready to charge. Timing, I have to wait and be patient. I pray that one day this sickness will be a blur as I build a fire in my heart and climb mountains with You. God has since given me many pictures of torches being handed to me in various ways. His faithfulness is astounding. Now they generally sit in my heart.

I cannot prove that Torchlight will manifest only that it is already there in the Spirit, every stage of the journey is Torchlight every encouragement from God and others is a step closer. Pressing in is the key, going forwards, allowing Him to lead and not attempting to run ahead no matter how tempting. He will only pull me back and it will be done in my own strength. I have nothing and I am no one but God can use those two wonderful things to bring about His purpose because ultimately it will be Him and His power that does it. He will show that although I am nothing I am everything in Him in his glory and precious timing as I push toward the goal and the upward call in Christ Jesus. Walking on water, walking on nothing as He leads the way. So Torchlight will manifest and come into being just as He said it would.

20.07.10

God asked me to draw a picture of a rainbow - rainbows as well as bees and butterflies have been extremely significant in my life. I had a real desire to draw this rainbow and to be obedient to this call. I felt it was going to be an advert for Torchlight at a later date but God's ways are not ours. I drew the picture and added some words underneath such as love peace and joy. Later that day I found myself studying the picture and God saying to me "What do you see?"

I said, " I see hope in the lives of people."

As time went on I began to feel the word hope was very significant and began a Bible study.

21.11.10

You initiated Lord a deep revelation of the word hope and I had a fairly restless night whilst you imprinted the word in my heart. I felt quite strongly that I was to share this important aspect of scripture with the television fellowship that I am part of. I did send in an email about it and the presenter picked up on the word, really bringing it to life. From the onset of the programme the word hope was featured and at the end someone sent in a poem about hope. I really feel You were speaking to us as a fellowship. I somehow believe that as I gave to others and shared the word of hope it actually brought hope to people and has sown a seed for the Torchlight ministry. "Beloved if God so loved us we also ought to love one another." *1 John 4:11*

I now know the true purpose of Torchlight Lord to bring this hope to others.

28.11.10

I want to thank You Lord. At church today I sought You, to worship You finding it a bit hard to enter in through being frazzled and tired from lack of sleep. The night before I had been overly concerned with this stage of Torchlight feeling it was moving into a practical/doing stage after two years of prayer and seeking. I began to feel I could not do it and that it was all too much and how would it happen, being only one person. Anyway I had a very strong impression that You were saying, "It was not in my strength but in Yours and that I could do all things through You, a frequent word from You Lord. I asked for a sign or word in church. During worship I was really impacted by the words on the screen 'I have set before you an open door.' *Rev 3:8.* I knew it was for me and I could not stop looking at it. That same morning a church leader had been given a picture of someone walking down a long road who had reached a point where the road was becoming thick and muddy. The person was stuck in themud, the walk was getting tougher and they felt they could not go on but God was saying, "just hold on, keep going." I put my hand up for prayer and two ladies prayed for me. I fell backwards and just cried and cried - I must have cried it all out. Thank You Lord, faithful God.

Last night Lord I prayed for another word from church, for a door to open for Torchlight. The lead minister prayed with me about the vision and said he had a picture of me at an airport going on a long journey and that there were many doors for me to go through. I was not getting on the plane but I had to go through a series of checks like passport control. You asked Lord if "I was willing to see out the whole journey?" Against all odds Lord, against all odds, I will never give up until I get to Torchlight. The leader prayed for the first door to open. He said that first I had to know the Father's love for myself. I cried at this point - again!

That afternoon You spoke to me at home. You said it would become a long haul flight and that I would have to plan my days around You. You said I cannot get distracted by the world. "Do not worry I am there right in the driving seat/cock pit. " I saw You Jesus with me in the plane. Later in worship I saw myself flying around in a little blue plane; the kind a baby would sit in at a fairground. You were there Lord, I was smiling like a child waving at their parents. I then realised You had been taking me on a baby journey, just looking around enjoying the ride. I then saw myself in a bigger more grown up plane as though I had progressed and was more confident, then I was in a jet; extremely powerful, then a rocket going up in a straight line to Father God. During this vision and time of worship I also grasped a sensation of the vast distance of heaven and how high the Father is - so very high and yet simultaneously You showed me how close He is, right within me. I heard You say, "He who has seen Me has seen the Father."

You are teaching me to fly, teaching me to walk and live by degrees just like the eagle. Thank You.

"Brethren count it all joy when you fall into various trials, knowing that the testing of your faith produces patience." James 1:2-3

03.12.10
A door opens

During prayer and worship at home today Lord I saw a picture of all sorts of people walking up a pathway some were hobbling and very poor, dragging themselves along looking desperate and some vile and unclean. You said to me "I want all to come - all. Before, You had given me a word from the Bible about being anointed to preach to the poor. I realised that we are all poor who do not know You. You then asked me to open the 'door of my heart' to receive all persons, to be willing to witness to all, to love all. You showed me this was the first door to open - the door of my heart and I had to be willing to obey before any more doors would open. For some time You have been teaching me to love, really love all people and to never judge.

"Beloved let us love one another, for love is of God and everyone who loves is born of God and knows God" *1 John 4.11.*

Praise You Lord You are always unexpected and we never know how You will work but when You do it is truly amazing. I prayed at this point for another door to open, of opportunity

Finding The love of the Father.
God is love, in this the love of God was manifested toward us

95

that God has sent His only begotten Son into the world that we might live through Him. In this is love not that we loved God but that he loved us and sent His Son to be the propitiation for our sins. 1.Jn 4:8

You will remember my pastor prophesied to me that I needed to find the love of the Father for myself. It makes sense to know we are really loved before we can carry that message to others. Before coming to Christ I really did not know what love was. I had witnessed failed relationships and broken friendships because of a root of rejection. When I very first walked into that little church all those years ago I was astounded by the people. I did not know that people like that existed. They reflected a genuineness, a love that I had never experienced. It was real and it shone out of their eyes. This was the light of Christ shining from their hearts. I remember the early days of my salvation and the problems it caused. Some thought I had been captured by a cult because of the radical transformation and the complete adoration I now felt for God. It is that adoration that now works through me to interpret the wonders of God and the truth of His existence to others.

I remember having a terrible conflict with somebody who was very angry at my salvation and love for God. Subsequently I felt very upset and angry myself. But now I was beginning to experience the love of God through others as a new Christian friend walked a fair distance to come and see me. She walked a long way to come and meet me where I was and helped me to understand forgiveness as she sat with me, as a friend. I was a baby Christian and that is fine. We have to begin the journey at the beginning. I cried as a baby and God heard me as a baby and sent me a spiritual mother to reassure me and build my faith. Now, more grown in the Lord I can go on to place *my* arm around a hurting world. This is the love of the Father. Yet I did not really experience the full love of the Father for many years. It was during a period of trauma and persistent spiritual attack I began to get a hold of the idea of the Father and His love for us. God had been impressing a verse from John on my heart, "Have I been with you so long Philip and yet you have not known Me." *John 14:9*

The Father was in Jesus all the time and He was desiring to reveal this to me. I had a particularly bad night and remembered the word. I called out "Abba, Abba Father!" He came. All my fears began to melt and turn to security as I sensed His great love and presence. It was as though this presence brought great revelation that the Father had always been with me and then I heard Him speak. "I have been waiting for you all your life when you would come to me, the Father. I have always been there, I know your heart and your love for Me. Hold on, hold on to the chariot reigns we are about to begin our journey and I will take you all the way to Torchlight. I will take you all the way and completely heal and restore you so that you will not know yourself as you walk on water as I walk right there beside you. Believe it with all your mind, all your heart and all your soul, it is the truth."

God does want to reveal Himself fully to us. We may know the sacrifice Jesus endured to save us from hell and a life of destruction; how He loved us so much that he chose to die for us, but for many people recognising the love of the Father can be a stumbling block. If people's earthly Fathers have failed them they can tend to believe they are not loveable and go on to fulfil a pattern of broken love and relationships, never finding true love or having any sense of worth. However our earthly Fathers are weak, they are human beings with failings and we need to cherish and forgive them whatever our experiences. God though is perfect and His love is just and faithful and holy. He loves us with that never - ending love and it is *Him* who sent His Son into the world because *He* first loved us.

"No one can come to Me unless the Father who sent Me draws him and I will raise him up at the last day. *John 6:44*

Father You draw us to Jesus so that we will go through Him and back to You. On the way through the door we are cleansed and forgiven.

You told me Lord "I would shine like a light in Your kingdom and when people are drawn to that light You will draw them to You through me as the Father drew people to You."

Torch

I spent a moment in the presence of the Lord. It is always worth it. Sometimes a moment is all God needs to show you something life changing. During this priceless gem of a moment I had a clear picture from God. There was a yak, Sherpa and some bundles all on a long mountainous road. God asked me "Who is your Yak and who is your Sherpa?" Several times He asked me the question. I perceived that the Sherpa was the Holy Spirit (a guide) and the yak was also the Holy Spirit (to carry). He was doing both these things in my life. I asked if I would climb the mountain alone. He told me that I would climb it alone but then people would be added. I asked if this picture was of Torchlight and God showed me the Sherpa handing me a torch and then planting it at the top of the mountain. All the heavy bundles I carried had to be thrown over the edge of the mountain en route - all trauma and unforgiveness, all that heavy baggage holding me up, anything left of self, all had to go. God is our Shepherd and the Holy Spirit is leading us along the journey and informing the way. God's word is a lamp to our feet and a light to our path. We need to know He is Shepherd and that He is sovereign. As our feet get lighter and we 'strip off every weight and the sin that so easily ensnares us,' nothing less than His best will do.
Your ears shall hear a word behind you saying this is the way walk in it.

Our great reward is serving the Lord, the great King. Moreover the realisation that this purpose is not for us but for Him and for others. Him because He deserves the glory even for life itself, for every breath we take, every beautiful sunset, the glimpse of a rainbow, a kind word spoken to us. It is about looking for service over self fulfilment and the many ways we can glorify Him. The road remains tough but we remember that is His promise, that the road *will* be difficult. Self still likes to pop up, but the reality of a life lived in Christ means we are dying to self and looking to the kingdom, the treasure, the pearl of great price. Other jewels now include: the knowledge that all is well, profound joy, peace that surpasses understanding, greatness in serving, true friendship and the treasure trove of wonders that God has yet to reveal. It does not take much to ponder these treasures and just how amazing God is. Can we fathom the Great King who has been from the beginning of time?

No one created Him, He just is. YHWH, the self - existent One. He has been from everlasting to everlasting. He has no beginning or end because He lives in eternity. He knew us before we were born and that He would need to send His Son Jesus to save us and bring us back to Him. He made everything and is able to know every thought of every person at the same time whilst holding the world together by His will. El Roi - the God who sees. He has given us the whole universe to enjoy, stars to gaze at, sunshine, rain, snow, hail, storms, the sea. We have the ability to survive using different talents and gifts to help the world function as a whole. We all have something, some wonderful gift that He has placed inside us for His purposes and His glory, we discover more as we ask Him and press in. He is a truly amazing God and thinking about these things serves only to draw us closer to Him.

Jess is lying on the sofa, soft, warm, secure like the valley. She thinks a lot about going. She prays, she hopes, she decides but finds herself wielding into the kitchen for sustenance, sustenance she doesn't need but it fills. Time goes on. Thankfully she is dying in this place of languid self indulgence. Turning, she feels a tightening in her stomach. There is no more time to waste. It's now or never because never may never come! Time is spiralling by and the calling stronger than ever before. His sleeping church is waking up and the body know He is on His way. Spirit to spirit He calls us. There is a prompting in the heart, in the Spirit, a sense of negligence and a desire to please Him more than ever before.

Breaking out now – the satisfaction – of the sound of the click of the remote control – turning off. The squeezing – of the pulling on of her boots and the sound of the door – closing. The road now thumping as she pounds the hard concrete treading the obscurity of the path – the outside foreboding but wonderful as she goes, in Him, in Christ.

Faith and Freedom

... and so it is that revelation comes. Not ours but His. I have found above all that the Word of God really is the absolute truth. Whether or not we have experienced all the truths for ourselves can never negate their reality. Jesus Himself is that truth, the path, the way and the door. He is truth just as He is love. His Word is inextricably bound with Him and cannot be separated. On my own journey God is drawing me ever closer to obey not just the Word itself but the requirements of the Word. We must be doers of the Word and not hearers only. The simplicity of the Word and its truth is leading me to recognise that yes there is a place for deep emotional healing through ministry; as this book frequently demonstrates, but more pertinently there is a place for just believing and having faith. Faith of itself to heal through the laying on of hands and to share His truth with others. Jesus simply healed through faith and very often required others' faith. The disciples followed suit. On my own journey I had been healed emotionally and delivered from much but recognised that the Word promotes an instant and full healing physically, even spiritually and emotionally. I would never doubt the Lord and His methods for taking people aside to clean them up on the inside and prepare them for service; all part of our walk. Which takes time and willingness.

Yet the scriptures also declare we can do His works and are to take up our cross and follow Him in these things. Literally taking His cross and truth out into the world and doing as He did. He will accompany us as we follow Him. The well-known 'lady with the issue of blood' was made whole by the healing touch of Jesus; made *whole*. Jesus often asked people what they wanted Him to do or to just believe. He seemed to be looking for faith to use, even though He Himself was Almighty God. The component or catalyst He used for healing was faith. Perhaps He didn't always heal the same way but He always used the same tools - faith, belief and authority. Demons fled at one word "Go!" People were raised from the dead and paralysis with one or two words, "wake up, get up, come out!" The disciples reiterated this example, "Get up, be healed!" And people did and were.

The truth is in the Word. It is for us too, as disciples of Christ. As we believe so we receive but we must go before the river can flow. Our faith can heal someone and raise the dead and much more as we step out and believe.

As God now encourages and pushes His church out in these last days we must expect a harvest. The signs will follow and they will alert people that the Kingdom of God really is at hand. This doesn't really work when we just tell people God loves them. There must be a demonstration of the Kingdom and power and a knowledge of REPENTANCE OF SINS to fully enter in and so we must take courage and speak the truth and go. Let us cast our bread upon the waters and after a few days it will return to us.

Bitter Sweets

As the plane slowly circled over the beautiful city my eyes widened at the sight before me. In the black of the night a million, twinkling lights shone out. Little slopes and houses steeped on hills; it was beautiful to behold. As we descended nearer I saw a miniature fair ground, little canopies strewn with lights twirled slowly around tipped to the side like little parasols. Tiny "big" wheels seemed to turn in story book fashion. I imagined happy smiles and little family gatherings, fathers holding children, mothers waving at their little ones on the rides. Perhaps a star struck couple sharing a look or some candy floss on the miniature big wheel.

Later on, during my trip a group of us visited a fairground - was it the same one?

At ground level the atmosphere was quite different. The rides appeared historic to say the least and health and safety was certainly not on the agenda. Where were the little parasols? Two of the young women in the group decided to throw caution to the wind and entertain a ride in a huge metal basin! At first there were little squeals of delight as the basin swayed softly from side to side, gently oscillating, but as momentum gathered the great basin quite suddenly tipped at an alarming 90 degree angle; swinging with greater and greater intensity tipping the riders upside down. Squeals turned to spine chilling screams as the women lost control, desperate to hold on as they slipped uneasily downwards. Praise God a wise worker who carried authority demanded the ride be stopped. Those poor women ghastly white and very shaken were released from a potential death trap.
Was it the same fairground?

A very skilful characteristic of the enemy's schemes is his ability to masquerade in varying shades of white. His tasty assortments in the "sweet shop" and playground of life know no bounds or clear analysis, just murky shades and shadows; until the One with authority shines a light on his schemes and steps in to stop the ride.

Remember "Be vigilant for your adversary the devil walks around like a prowling lion seeking whom he may devour."

Stepping onto the coach my heart raced with excitement. Outside the air was thick, scorched. At times it was overpowering, heady. My sandals felt right against the hot, dusty road. Life was different here, people carried great packages, full of food. They were huge, white, tightly packed sacks, not like anything an English person would transport on a coach, but then, was there a shortage in the lives of these local people? Women seemed to scurry at times or at best keep their heads low, wearing the traditional hijab. There was a great sense of the gender divide. Would it have been like this in Israel or Samaria in Jesus' time? Women who were considered lower than men and burdened with routine chores?

Why didn't I tell them?

There was though a sense of humility here, a sagacity, a peaceful coexistence that may quite suddenly erupt into warfare. This created a tension not so apparent in our society. One must live here with a sense of polar divide; relying on one's friends and family as the source of constancy.

The roads were long now as we embarked on a twenty four hour trip. The scenery was incredible as it slowly changed from lush green to brown to red. Hot, dusty, arid. An occasional tank or army vehicle rolled on by or could be seen in the distance amid the stark military presence, soldiers menacing, guns in their hands. Looking, always looking. I knew I was far from home and the seeming safety of a more stable culture, far from everything I knew. Yet excitement filled my very being as the coach rolled on taking me further into unstable territory and heightened risk.

We are winding through a valley now lush, green, early morning dew reflecting a misty, chalky quality of the very present dawn. On both sides were mountains, some brownish some green, water sparkled and trees bowed as though eager to drink in the fresh rivers of water. Slowly heads popped up as one by one passenger's began stretching and rising up in their well - worn seats. As they awoke a sense of anticipation filled the air we knew our long trip was coming to an end.

As I walk through the door I am asked to remove my shoes. Women eagerly wait to meet me, hands extend, compliments flow. I understand a few words. I am received with great honour. We take tea together, black, strong and although it is a familiar convention I am now traversing new territory, fresh, undiscovered waters, the family. Family is everything here. Roots to survival lay in the home. Mother is queen. For a strictly divided society the mothers are pure matriarchs, disciplining their families well. The female siblings clean the house most days from top to bottom, rugs scrubbed and hung out to dry, floors spotless. If they aren't cleaning their own houses they clean each other's. This isn't wrong just different, perhaps it is good. Meals are prepared artistically with faithful resolve; made from scratch - no packets. Women collectively cook, sharing the unity of bonding together in genuine sisterhood. They welcome me, they appear kind, gentle. How the families, brim with enthusiasm as they soak in each other's company. In the winter months they share food huddling by great, metal fires disdaining the chill outside. Such richness in sharing.

Yet would they step aside? Would they dare to be different, share a converse opinion or unpick their lot? Am I wrong in my observations? Do they have it right? Have their lives been so ordered and set that there is no opinion or concept of challenge? I only know that Jesus came to set the captives free and to heal the brokenhearted. I see captivity at times but it is silent, in the eyes. Perhaps it is a reflection of my own at this time. If I shared my broken heartedness with my husband in this culture would I be beaten for it, or am I so saturated with the media that I am suspicious of these people's bonded lives? It is truly beautiful how the sexes have their appointed roles here, something Biblical in terms of women tending the home and raising children and how these things alongside a gentle and quiet spirit are beautiful to the Lord. There are echoes of my own life experience where being a mum and homemaker have brought great joy. One wonders if it is actually less of a demand to stay home without choice than it is to hold down a career, be a mum and tend the house like many western women. The virtuous woman celebrated in Proverbs would challenge this concept. Of importance is our obedience to the Lord where does He want us to be? How will He use our given circumstances to change lives? There will sometimes be a bumpy ride for the Christian woman in terms of context. Are we in subjection? Are we comparable? There are no such questions here? I come, I go. Similarly as East meets West   two great, disconnected ships converge momentarily before they silently sail apart. Could I have left eternal bounty for these people before changing course? If Jesus were here how would it differ? Would He sail away or would He meet these women head on, at right angles kissing our differences goodbye. Lives certainly hold together with His appearing but to live and breathe these people they seem to have an authentic connection in the family and social context. I am not being ignorant to the subversion of abuse, fear and control imposed on women and actually prevalent in every society, and certainly am not agreeing with any false religion, but have we got it completely right in our hedonistic culture? For the Christian our only real difference is Jesus, but what a difference He makes? In essence there is only one God and all we need is to trust in the Lord. He Himself is an ocean of faith - for us.

If I had shared Christ's grace and beauty with these women, if I knew the language, if I had looked for a way. I think there would be a gentle instilling of peace that surpasses understanding and a sisterhood based on friendship and not institution. But none of us can judge, who are we to judge another? In this season of my life I believe they had much right and my life was mostly wrong. Yet praise God there is no condemnation, our role is to bring Christ and tell the truth in love and then look to our own healing and correction as well as to others.   If we miss the boat let's quickly jump on another one. It is true that God has a divine plan already unfolding in the background and our perceived lateness may just be God's providence. God certainly turns all things for good. Leaving behind this people group that I struggled to witness to I now have insight into a hardworking culture where Jesus is unknown and the idea of embracing another God terrifies them. People here are survivors, surviving extremes of weather and extremes politically. They have suffered degrees of persecution and discrimination but they *are fighters. They are wonderful people with strong women completely dedicated to the life they have been given. Yes they lack choice but do they want it yet, would they know what to do with it? Now I can pray specifically for individuals. For Christ to come and pour out His Spirit, for revival, for salvation.*

Christ in us the hope of glory. May we bring Him to the nations but may we meet in the middle and learn from one another as we bring Christ and exchange wisdom.

I experienced the countryside and the little villages where whole families communed together, growing food to sell in the towns. People here were busy and industrious. Women would hoist up their skirts and make cheese. Great slabs bashed and rolled on the ground, years of tradition passed down. Survival. As I ventured further into the ways of this land; into the city, I desired more to be with my God and to find Him fully once more in all His glory. He wasn't far away.

In the city the air was greatly polluted, cars dominated this highly populated place and much time on my trip was spent here in this metropolis. Like any city it offered good and bad elements. Things were becoming familiar now. There was the bridge that crossed the centre of a huge, busy road. Traffic here was really intense. Horns frequently blasting, manic drivers speeding along; seat belts, speed limits seemed an unknown entity in this chaotic thoroughfare. At least two people I met had crashes during my stay, one died, he was a taxi driver and the road his livelihood. Conflict remained, with different tensions here. A sense of freedom prevailed. People smoked cigarettes wherever they wanted even when serving behind counters. They smiled and jostled about interacting in wonderful collective ways, always listening and allowing to speak. What were they saying? Oftentimes people would interpret but you never really knew. How important words are, how important is what we say and understand, it shapes our whole being. At family gatherings I could never be sure; were they talking about life? Politics? Their God? People roamed as in any city but usually with a great deal of purpose. They toiled hard, rushing about working eighteen hour shifts.

Opportunists - in the rain, little stalls selling umbrellas appeared, in the snow, hats, scarves and gloves. Yet there issued an undercurrent, a tension suggestive of a place that wasn't really free. Small children sold tissues on the bridge, they themselves freezing cold, noses frequently running with no kind parent to wipe them. I loved the bridge, it gave a familiarity, a crossing point, a landmark, but I also dreaded it. Police carried guns. Mothers would beg here with babies on their laps, laid out cold, motionless, rigid, were they drugged? As you drew near they would wave the baby's bottle with a contrived spirit to catch your attention. I saw a little old lady curled up so small, posed in an artistic, coiled like position her arm central pushed behind her, facing upwards to collect tokens from passers' by. Head bowed low to reflect deep sorrow or possibly shame. Within a stone's throw another lady, evidently her aid, watching, learning.

Why didn't I tell them?

Cafes were my stronghold in the city, I felt safe amidst the friendly workers. The food, spicy yet insipidly lukewarm offered a consistency and a vague reassurance that all was well. I will remember the teeming people, dark skinned and slim, no obesity here - no time. The interesting shops showcasing glimmering glass and flickering shapes. The dodgy food and variety of life. The poor, abandoned women with no hope of a future but to beg. The sorrowful street children cold and neglected. Furthermore the wonderful families that would share their last piece of bread with you and welcome you into their homes to sleep on their floors or share their company. The dedicated young women worshipping with an earnest sincerity - their god. No way out of their communities, no choices. Yet juxtaposed, sharing a sisterhood most western women could only dream of. Mostly I will remember my Lord who kept me in provision and safety at a time when I was far from my walk but desperate for Him. Will you take me back one day Lord? Will I again cross that bridge bringing Your Word to a lost and hungry city, exchanging my trepidation for a Bible and my reserve for the King?

So began my true journey with the King.

My Israel My Israel

Dedication

For Amber

Contents

Promise

Isaiah 27

The time is coming when Jacob's descendants will take root.
Israel will bud and blossom
and fill the whole earth with fruit.
Has the Lord struck Israel
as he struck her enemies?
Has he punished her
as he punished them?
No,
but he exiled Israel to call her to account.

She was exiled from her land
as though blown away from a storm in the East.
The Lord did this to purge Israel's wickedness
to take away all her sin.

...the people are like the dead branches of a tree
broken off and used for kindling beneath the cooking pots.
...yet the time will come when the Lord will gather them -
from the Euphrates River in the East from the Brook of Egypt
in the West. In that day the great trumpet will sound. Many
who were dying in exile in Assyria and Egypt will return to
Jerusalem to worship the Lord on His Holy mountain.

*Jerusalem will become a refuge for those who escape; it will be
a Holy place*
*And the people of Israel will come back to reclaim their
inheritance...*

*...then saviours will come to Mount Zion to judge the
mountains of Esau and the Kingdom shall be the Lord's.*
Obadiah 21

God's Word says we are to pray for the peace of Jerusalem. Some time ago I began to have a real sense of compassion for Jewish people. I couldn't really understand why but I felt a depth of love for them and for Israel that I had never experienced. God works things together and He does it little by little and before long I found myself in a prayer group for Israel and began to assimilate an understanding of Israel past and present almost by osmosis. I began a yearning to go to Jerusalem and to experience all things Jewish. Perhaps it was the knowledge that our wonderful Saviour is Jewish or perhaps it was purely God's will for me to pray for His people. Yet more than that I believe these really are the last days and that alongside the Jewish people themselves making Aliyah there is a calling on more and more Christians to pray into this wonderful mystery of Jesus coming back and His people being prepared in the land of His choosing to await their King.

Miracles have arisen out of the dust. The dark days of the Holocaust that killed six million Jews including one and half million children have been converted into a regeneration of not only a Jewish homeland, but the return of thousands upon thousands of Jewish people that are compelled to return by the call of the Almighty in their hearts.

Cutting back the tree has only served to strengthen the root and the scattered remnant of seeds will flourish by the powerful hand that leads them. A greater miracle will emerge; leaping out from the pages of God's Word, as more and more Jewish people receive the knowledge of who their Saviour is.

The book of Ezekiel decrees that God will bring armies up against Israel in the last days. He will put hooks in their noses and bring them up from the North and lead them out with a mass of arsenal and weaponry. They will be led out and pulled by *Him*. Sometimes when we look to the Bible and see how the world is being staged for Jesus second coming and the great battle of the end we can forget it is His divine plan to bring the nations against Israel where Jesus Himself will reign and His saints with Him. When we pray for the peace of Jerusalem we usher in the plans of God.

Yet in the Word of God; even beyond established prophecy there lies a pure illustration of hope. The account of Noah and the ark; in Genesis, conceals some particularly poignant and hidden elements. These deeper dimensions reveal interweaving and beautifully crafted promises connecting with other elements of scripture in a remarkable way. There is much to reveal the loving heart of the Father. Before He announced the imminent flood that would wipe out the entire world; which may seem a harsh and excessive extreme, the Bible states God was grieved in His heart and sorry He had made man. He remains the Creator, the Potter and we are the clay. He is sovereign. Yet God has a way of retaining a remnant, a seed for the future and 'Noah found grace in God's eyes.'

God had commanded this honourable man to bring his family and the selected animals to shelter. Not only would it be a passage across deep, deep waters but a passage of great faith where Noah would encounter God's supreme faithfulness.

The torrents of water would eventually cease allowing God's hand to bring the ark to safety and beyond! Nevertheless things got decidedly worse before they got better as the waters prevailed and continued to do so. Even when the ark landed on Ararat there was a long way to go; exiting the ark, the logistics of the animals and the people, how would they get down the mountain? Noah and his wife were not young and not all animals are designed to climb. Yet significant for the Christian; we are told that tribulation sharpens our faith. In fact it defines it, giving God access to deeper and deeper channels within, like the waters of Noah. It is the *climbing* of the mountain or in Noah's case; its great descent, that shapes us. The difficulties, the horror and pains of life. The tragedies, the issues and problems that frequent the lives of all of us, it is these that connect us to Him and moreover to ourselves. For Noah, deep literally called unto deep as his own soul and those of his family were entrusted firmly in the hands of God. Likewise we are encouraged on our walk not to look at the waves or the storms but to keep our eyes on Jesus as Noah kept His eyes on the Lord and His promise.

Can we imagine what the journey was like for Noah? We know He was a just man, perfect in his generation, this in itself quite remarkable. Can we imagine *being* Noah and told to build an ark for the saving of our families? He must have moved in great faith; believing God and trusting in His word to him and the promise that would follow. Noah remains the embodiment of a faithful servant sparking great faith in the generations to come. This man; advanced in years, received instruction on how to build the ark, followed this through and had tremendous conviction that God really would destroy the whole world but also that he and his family would be saved.

The passage on the waters must have been truly horrendous:
Waves booming and rolling as the ark ascended high above the earth, continually elevating to greater and greater heights. The terror as the 'fountains of the great deep' were gushing out pushing the ark higher, soaring and crashing into the waves. The windows of heaven thrown open, relentless, pouring rain, unstoppable. The terrors of the churning ocean only to be darkly imagined by the courageous passengers within; surrounded by dense wood and unremitting darkness. A terrifying journey of intense, explicit fear.

Or was it?
Could it have been a matchless challenge beyond compare where Noah almost navigated his way through the storms? Literally cutting through adversity and the tight walls of testing. Did his faith reach unassailable heights and unparalleled depths of expectation? The great ark would have been tiny in such a vast ocean, an ocean that filled the world. One could picture a tiny submarine weaving in and out of a Thunderbirds scene. So small, but inside the ark faithful Noah, his eyes fixed, soaring to pinnacles of trust as he soldiered on through the depths of the waves, the invincible captain of an infallible ship, designed by Almighty God, never

to fail?

And so for the disciple, are our minds set like a flint? Do we *know* God has already chartered our path? Do we know and trust in the integrity of our Lord? Jesus the faithful servant and 'Ark.'

Can we imagine where Noah's thoughts were in all this? I believe he was steadfast reflecting his noble character. Negativity on the ark would have proved deadly and may have caused great fear. There would be a responsibility of *remaining* in faith leading to hope. One only has to look at the mind blowing statement from Helen Keller; who was deaf, blind and mute, "life is a daring adventure or nothing," to understand that life is more than we can see, hear or touch. Is our passage of faith a challenging adventure or a fearful expression?
"Hope in the Lord for I shall yet praise Him."

How did it feel to push open the window of the ark? How vast was it? It is nice to imagine the fresh air penetrating the length and breadth of the ark. Little animal noses and snouts' lifting upwards sniffing this curious yet familiar smell. The smell of waste and dead air; dank, possibly stomach churning, would be refreshed bringing life and hope for the confined animals. Was there something new in the air; was it still consumed with droplets of water?

Leaving the ark must have been a tumultuous enterprise. There is no indication that God tells Noah to open the window and send out a raven and a dove. It seems Noah is using the gift of reason to work out the next step. Perhaps God is gradually edging back as Noah progressively takes little steps towards freedom? Has God loosened the reigns, encouraging Noah to make informed choices, to step out into the brave new world? Guiding the animals to their eventual habitations and leading Noah to build an alter to glorify his faithful God whilst never loosening the reigns of His Spirit, ever drawing.

There is so much to symbolise all that the Lord is in this

invaluable description of the flood. We have God's promise of life and safety, a new start. God's assurance that He would keep His word and His further promise to never again flood the whole world; confirmed by eternal covenant. However; as indicated, this wonderful passage contains some very hidden dimensions unveiling some interesting parallels. We have worship; where Noah on reaching safety, honours the Lord, building an alter and seemingly expressing a knowledge of burnt offering. The killing of the birds would have incorporated an element of blood sacrifice igniting a remote ember of the cross; glimpses of the King. The word covenant has a root meaning 'flesh cut away.' Just As the Saviour's flesh was torn away and His blood poured out, He became the fulfilment of the covenant. Jesus saved His creation a second time, making a way for *all* to come. Noah's ark was a box symbolising a carrier, a place to keep something safe or hidden or a means to transport something. The Ark of the Covenant was also a box to transport and keep hidden. The root word for ark (of covenant) means to pluck or gather, strongly akin to Noah's being plucked out and kept in safety in a different kind of ark. This root also represents a chest or coffin which when translated to Noah could be a place of waiting or holding whilst rebirth commenced on leaving the ark. Peter describes baptism as an antitype of this reflecting the washing in water, *1 Peter. 3.21.* Noah's ark kept within it the righteous remnant, outside the flood fulfilling the consequence of man's sin. When Jesus was nailed to the cross He kept within Him the sin of the world washing it in His precious blood to emanate outwards the glorious salvation and rivers of living water counter posing the killing waters of Genesis. The Ark of the Covenant also kept within it something very Holy and very righteous and God Himself dwelt there. The dove returning to the ark points to the Holy Spirit and the olive leaf symbolic of peace.

Interestingly Moses was also saved in a mini ark as he was hidden in the Nile and brought to a place of safety. God's excellent providence restoring him to his mother to be nourished by her, undetected by pharaoh's wife. His name carrying the meaning 'drawn out' whispers again of the safety of leaving the ark and being rescued alongside whispers of election.

Of great significance was the rainbow also referred to as an arc. The root meaning for rainbow in Noah, is pertaining to a bending bow as of an archer, symbolic of God's grace. Could it even point to Jesus and the glorious prospects to come? Was God revealing even in these the earliest of times His perpetual blessing and the glory of the New Jerusalem? In Zechariah God prophesies that He is bending Judah His bow. This great bow bent and fixed set to conquer and point towards a future of hope. 'He has fitted that bow with Ephraim' representing fruitfulness. Judah represents praise and perpetuates the generational line of Jesus who is also celebrated as the 'Lion of the tribe of Judah.' This has a strong prophetic edge where Jesus will return as the conqueror. He came as the Lamb and will return as the Lion. Jacob, in blessing his sons, refers to Judah as a lion's whelp (cub) pointing again to Jesus as the personification. Furthermore the sceptre begins in Judah's hand and remains until Shiloh comes, our wonderful Saviour who then passes it to His kingdom and those that will enter in. The animals would have been sovereignly restrained in the ark where the lion and lamb would dwell close by. Both symbolic of the authority of the Lord and the gentleness of the lamb. In the age to come Isaiah prophecies that the lion will lay down with the lamb, peace established for evermore - the New Jerusalem.

Blessing and honour and glory and power be to Him who sits on the throne and to the lamb forever.
Revelation 5:13

On leaving the ark Noah is told to be fruitful and multiply. When God calls His people back home to Zion He says the seed shall be prosperous and the vine shall give its fruit and He shall cause the remnant of this people to possess all these. Another remnant, another 'new' land. Eventually a lifting of the curse and the promise of blessing. "Sing and rejoice oh daughter of Zion! For behold I am coming and I will dwell in your midst, says the Lord. Many nations shall be joined to the Lord in that day, and they shall become My people and I will dwell in your midst. Then you will know that the Lord of hosts has sent Me (Jesus) to you. And the Lord will take possession of Judah as His inheritance in the Holy Land and will again choose Jerusalem." *Zechariah 2.*

Now Jesus has broken down the middle wall of separation and we shall all be one in Him, no Jew, no Greek just one body and all will eventually come to Zion, where we will serve and reign with Almighty God. God will once more remember His people and call His people home, gathering His people into a land that appears so unstable so threatened at this time but will become the ruling city of the world where peace and rest will finally enter in, the final ark of safety for God's people. Jerusalem, the Holy City reverberating down the years from David to Yeshua, person to person, city to city, sword to sword. He takes His children very seriously cursing those who curse them and blessing those who bless them. He encourages us to pray for the peace of Jerusalem and indicates strongly that those who touch them touch the apple of His eye, literally poking Him in the eye. All pointing to the promises to come.

In revelation the rainbow around God's throne depicts an Iris and can be compared with the eye that reflects colour. There are connotations of watching and remembering when we see that great arc in the sky. The rainbow around the throne is emerald in appearance which has a root 'nopek' meaning to glisten or shine. In Ezekiel, the appearance of the Lord on the throne is compared to 'a rainbow in a cloud on a rainy day, 'this was the appearance of the brightness around it, the appearance of the likeness of the glory of the Lord.' In scientific terms rainbows are formed by droplets of water reflecting in the sun; water, indicative of those rivers of living water and light, perfect just like the Lord shining out. The bow has seven colours God's number of perfection and completion. This in itself is such a sign of God's presence and holiness. God could have created more than seven colours but He is perfect and His ways are perfect and His will must be done at all times. In His precise timing He left something beautiful for Noah and for us. The very name, Noah means resting place or quiet just like our wonderful

Lord and the Holy Spirit. As Noah rested in the ark so we can rest in our beautiful Jesus.

Was it any mistake that those set to conquer the new world were explicitly chosen? They were all couples, married to fulfil multiplication. The name Japheth carries the meaning of expansion, to open out. This is exactly how God led His people to expand and conquer and eventually inherit the land promised to them. Shem carries the meaning of authority and honour. He is the seed of Israel; the future of the saints, another resting place.

Over eons of time the promises of God are being fulfilled as they flow outwards from the matrix of His heart, drawing inwards and ever narrowing. Coming to fruition down the generations because His Word never fails, and will culminate in the New Jerusalem residing in eternity where every tear will be wiped away. God will place a crown of life on our heads and we will know all things. The trumpet will blow and the sound of the shofar will serve as a resonating reminder of a God who cannot lie as He comforts His people Israel.

Dedication

In sorrow and repentance for the many beautiful and courageous Jewish people that lost their lives during the Holocaust and to those that survived

Ezekiel 37

The hand of the Lord was upon me and He brought me out
by the Spirit of the Lord and set me in the middle of a valley;
it was full of bones. He led me back and forth among them
and I saw a great many bones on the floor of the valley, bones
that were very dry. He asked me "son of man can these
bones live?"
I said "Sovereign Lord you alone know." Then He said to me,
"prophesy to these bones and say to them. 'Dry bones hear
the word of the Lord!' This is what the Sovereign Lord says to
these bones: "I will make breath enter you and you will come
to life. I will attach tendons to you and make flesh come
upon you and cover you with skin; I will put breath in you
and you will come to life. Then you will know that I am the
Lord."
So I prophesied as I was commanded. And as I was
prophesying there was a noise, a rattling sound and the
bones came together, bone to bone. I looked and tendons
and flesh appeared on them and skin covered them. Then He
said to me, " Prophesy to the breath; prophesy, son of man
and say to it; This is what the Sovereign Lord says: Come
from the four winds, O breath, and breathe into these slain.
That they may live." So I prophesied as He commanded me,
and breath entered them; they came to life and stood up on
their feet - a vast army. Then He said to me; "son of man
these bones are the whole house of Israel. They say, 'our
bones are dried up and our hope is gone; we are cut off.'
Therefore prophesy and say to them: 'This is what the
Sovereign Lord says: Oh My people, I am going to open your
graves and bring you up from them; I will bring you back to
the land of Israel. Then you My people, will know that I am
the Lord, when I open your graves and bring you up from
them. I will put my Spirit in you and you will live, and I will
settle you in your own land. Then you will know that I the
Lord have spoken and I have done it declares the Lord.' "

Treasures in the Darkness

I have been really touched by the focus on Israel and the Jewish people these last few years. There is a return to persecution and with the rise of Islam and the spread of Jew hatred across the nations once more notions of war loom heavily in the background.

As the Word of God reveals we; the Gentiles, that are in Christ, have been grafted into the vine. The Jewish people are the original branches and Jesus is the Vine. We were grafted in due to Israel's unbelief and are provoked through God's Word to be *moving them to jealousy* that they may be grafted back in. We are all one in Christ, no Jew, no Greek but many Jewish people have not had this revelation yct. They are veiled/blinded to this truth until 'the fulness of the gentiles has come in' and then all Israel will be saved. If we curse them we will be cursed and if we bless them we will be blessed.

It is the greatest honour to be grafted in to these wonderful people and into the Kingdom of our Lord who Himself was and is Jewish. We are the people of faith because in Abraham all the nations will be blessed and the Jewish people are the seed of Abraham. The enemy of our souls also wants to annihilate the Jews. This was reflected historically through Haman, Herod and Hitler amongst the many other enemies of God including Canaan, Esau, Ishmael and many others whose descendants are still contending for Israel's destruction. The church have had a part in this in the past and still have through the application of the BDS movement and the misunderstanding of the centrality of Israel and God's chosen people. The misconception of Replacement Theology has done much to misinform the church and to damage Israel both now and in the past.

Prayer
Lord as the nations and enemies of Israel rise up once more attempting the extermination of Your chosen people, raise up another Esther. Lord we know it is written and prophesied that You will 'put hooks in their noses' but Lord protect Your people in these last days. There is a seeping darkness echoing the schemes and pervading undertones of the past.

Raise up a church who will stand with Your people in the very midst of prophecy. Perhaps Lord we; the church, are here for such a time as this.

The short story that follows has been inspired by a deep sadness for the plight of the Jews and the devastating effects of Hitler's 'Final Solution' towards the end of the second world war. This inspiration leaves one yearning to have been a vehicle for the saving of the people not only physically from the horrors of neglect and starvation but to bring YESHUA'S saving grace amongst His chosen Jewels.

Edyta

Stepping over the rubble, Edyta entered the Ghetto. Her hands tucked tightly in her heavy, black coat felt safe in the deep, woollen pockets. Outside and around her the air was stark. A deathly stillness filled the gloomy, stinking air. The head scarf tied several times around her neck offered a meagre barrier to the intense cold. Yet the coldness she felt in her hands and feet helped her to feel alive inside and ignited a glint of warmth flickering albeit uneasily in her heart. She thought of her sister dragging her black coat around the back yard and laying it in the pig sty overnight. She had gone without sleep, had little food and not washed for many weeks. She must fit in. She could not stand out.

Her feet slipped constantly over the incessant debris of brick and rubble, sharp pieces of stone gashed her legs as they rolled over her feet but eventually she approached the filthy street. German guards milling about filled her with terror.

There he was, the little Jewish boy. He did not seem to have moved since yesterday. Lying on his side, cold and rigid perhaps he was dead. Was she too late? Keeping her head low she entered the street. She shuffled as if lame, as if old as if maneuvered by the very hand of God.

Out of nowhere a car skidded. She came crashing down her body rolling to the ground. She felt no pain as yet as she rolled closer to the little boy. An angry German, standing in the moving vehicle; shouted curses of Jewish pigs, aimed his gun and attempted to shoot her prostrate body but he failed and alarmingly the vehicle kept going. She was hurt now, she was injured but no matter, to them she was Jewish and she was very close to her prize.

Crawling slowly and deliberately towards him she felt the coldness of the filthy street. She felt exposed and afraid but her eyes and heart were fully alert and focused on the boy. At length she was able to lay right behind him. As she drew close the smell was overwhelming.   Speaking in her native Polish she whispered in his ear. "I'm going to help you." She sensed movement, indistinct and minimal but it *was* movement. She whispered again, "what is your name?" The boy could not move, he really was dying. Slipping her hand into her pocket she retrieved the little flask of water she had carefully carried. Pulling him around to face her she commenced to pour it into his mouth. Choking and coughing on the paltry trickle brought him a little to his senses and he seemed to whisper "Yosef." Pouring in more water she pushed the flask tightly into his hand with the carrot she had faithfully kept in her pocket. "Go to the stones," she whispered before feeling a sharp kick in her back. Another German shouting and kicking her until she moved. Looking to the floor she scurried away scared and terrified. Yet somehow once more, she reached the rubble. Had she been intercepted, she didn't know? She hastened back across the churning brick and fell almost headlong into a small dugout. Here she waited until after dark and crept silently into the woods. Miraculously unseen.

She did not enjoy her breakfast the next day. Staring absently outside she looked at her porridge with a guilt that pierced her very being. The meagre supplies they had were still abundantly more than many in the Ghetto could ever hope for. Standing at the window she felt pain in her body. Her legs and back hurt beyond measure but it was a reminder. The reminder she needed to forget her own suffering and focus on Yosef. She had not really understood how she had got away, how she had got home the night before and whether she could make it back. God willing. Had Yosef even understood her, did he keep hold of the water, the carrot? She didn't know. Falling to her knees and disregarding her food she sought peace and protection from a faithful God.

She had figured it might take him a week to reach the rubble, if he even lived another day? After two days she was compelled. She knew she must go. Her and Anna made ready. Clutching the old wheelbarrow covered with straw and blankets they stole off into the night. As Edyta approached the stones cold and alone, her heart beat loudly in her chest. She felt she could hear every beat and her throat filled with sand and gravel. With shallow, rapid breathing and shaking hands she felt her way once more across the stones. Thankfully the timing was good and dusk was descending rapidly providing a milky covering. It was almost curfew. Through terror and weakness all she had was the next step but that was enough. Her eyes darted about surveying the street, capturing every position of the guards. She thought about her very life and whether she would be caught but these thoughts quickly faded as she suddenly spotted Yosef. With a sharp intake of breath she walked towards him. He had made it a little closer, praise God. He was still laying down perhaps from sustained exhaustion. However he looked just the same. Edyta paused for a moment behind him then abruptly and courageously picked him up. Carrying him in her arms she edged towards the rubble. There was no weight to him. She guessed he was about nine but who could tell with his withered body.

Somewhere she heard dogs, and noisy soldiers but she kept going. Perhaps they hadn't seen her. Stopping suddenly in relief she bundled him into the little bunker with her before escaping into the woods. Anna waiting with the barrow acted quickly as both women shook from the cold and the shock. Still they heard dogs, still they heard shouting and dull gunfire but they kept going pushing their prize deep into fear and deep into freedom. They had never been more afraid or more determined but they kept going.

Back at the farmhouse the women worked hurriedly. Reality hit them as sharply as the cold morning air. Edyta had managed to exchange her threadbare, 'Jewish' slippers for the now sturdy but dew graced boots hidden in the barrow where Yosef lay. Throughout the journey they had fed him water and strained vegetable juice. The mashed cornmeal stuffed in their own pockets sufficed for the sisters through the night. Much of the ten mile journey had encompassed a long, cold river walk amid the frequent breaks in a vain attempt to scupper any scent. They were cold and they were wet.
Quickly and efficiently reliving each determined drill Mikel helped the women carry Yosef into the chamber beneath the cellar. Mikel had managed to create an adequate supply of light and air. They laid him on the bed, covering it with the

straw and blankets and there proceeded to pray.

For two weeks the exhausted sisters fed him like a baby, strained juice leading to porridge three times a day. They'd had to sacrifice much of their own supplies which wasn't easy especially as their daily lives needed to appear the same. They nursed him and encouraged him day by day waiting for signs of revival.

Yosef

Yosef's eyes were blurred he had no true feeling in his body. He was a living-dead person. He only felt cold, motionless as dark thoughts permeated his young mind. But now through the watery blur he could vaguely see the little cross shape. It glinted gold hanging around the neck of the black shadow that fed him and covered him whenever he was cold. As the days grew he saw that cross more clearly shining like a little light in the darkness. He began to wait for it. It dangled in front of him adorning the black shadow that was also becoming lighter and beginning to fill the room and his thoughts, with new life. Gradually he grew stronger and began to feel this new life in his little bones and feet. He wanted to stretch his legs now, to turn his head to feel the ground beneath him and to reach out to that golden light. Reaching forward he held out his arm and held the little cold shape in his hand. Witnessing the joy of the beholder he forced a smile on a sunken face and felt the beginning of life.

Miriam

Miriam lay on the plank she had been given as a bed. Her hair and body crawling with lice. Beside her at least another fifty women. Perhaps fifty above and several hundred more in the same room. She tried to recall her home but it kept fading as her thoughts continually returned to her son Yosef. Her mind had seemingly lost its former function where only thoughts of Yosef prevailed. Sometimes the weakness she felt was like death, her hopelessly limp yet terrifyingly rigid body had become one with the plank. Bare, desolate and dead. Yet she could not die, all the time he may be living, she could not die. Her teeth now misshapen, loose and discoloured brought a painful discomfort as she remembered the boy. She would be woken at five and labour until six; if she made it. She would have a little food perhaps dried fish bone soup and some water; just enough to keep her marginally alive. Her thoughts were so mushy now and complicated. She dreamed of death and sometimes her garden that once was.

Mikel
Mikel was too strong to go to the Ghetto, he would be spotted in a moment. It had to be Edyta. Now their plan had worked and Yosef their prize. He was getting strong now and played around the house. It was a risk but he needed to be moved so that Edyta could return - for another. He reflected over his own escape. Yes he was strong, clever but so were many others in the ghetto. Was it God's hand that he should get away.

In the fog of shadows and deep darkness Miriam lay. On her shoulder a sharp tap. Too weak to look she closed her eyes. There He was. She'd glimpsed Him before. In a shadow? In a dream? Now His beauty was filling her mind. The veiled Man with the white covering. He became brighter, her heart alive and alert to every breath. Throwing off chords and bands of death her eyes saw a shape. A small, golden, glinting cross and the smile of Yosef; his name written across it. The beautiful Man faded from view but her heart remained fully with Him. As He slowly pulled away she felt chords of love binding her to Him as He disappeared into the darkness leaving His light.
"I am Yeshua I am that Light."

Mikel remembered the day he had arrived at the farmhouse. The fear on the sister's faces quickly changing to concern as he had collapsed in the doorway. How they had fed him and told him of their Lord. Could this be the One he had heard of?

Miriam had gained favour these last weeks. She knew not how but the supernatural strength Yeshua had given her caused her to now care for her sisters in the camp. She had gained a little daily fish and water from the guard Adel, she even knew his name. She had not noticed him before but he was certainly different. Miriam chose one of the sisters, Gerda who was old and crippled and dying and decided to share a mouthful of the fish with her each day. She could not give more as she needed the strength to help. Each evening Miriam ministered to the old lady, singing praises to God and telling her about Yeshua. On the day Gerda drew her last breath Miriam became one with her, filled with joy and a love beyond measure, beyond comprehension. Miriam's last days would glorify her wonderful Yeshua as she brought His name to her sisters and increased in strength and vitality; filled with His light.

Adel

Adel stood in the corridor. The filthy stench of the Jewish women caused him to retch and gag. He could not bear it. He hated being a soldier, being a German. Before he had seemed desensitised, seeing these women as non- human, as rats and pigs as they all had. He had no qualms about destroying them; keeping them penned up in this hell-hole where they belonged. But now he wasn't sure. Recently something had happened, he knew his eyes had been touched and he could see something different. The lady, Miriam had touched his heart - he hated himself. What had happened to him? Perhaps he was losing his mind as he found himself sharing his food with a Jew. Yet somehow his mind didn't feel lost.

Adinah

In the ghetto Adinah had seen the mysterious woman in the black coat. She had seen her snatch the little boy and escape over the rubble. Where had she taken him? She'd watched her disappear into the night. This strange lady had given her hope. Sitting on the cold street, holding her baby, Elia in her arms she reflected in the darkness of the night. How could she have carried that boy alone? How had she passed the guards? Why hadn't she returned? Elia was so small now, so helpless. Adinah had almost given up hope of her survival, until now.

Day after day she had sat on these streets and nobody gave them anything. Even the public water tap was getting clogged and monopolised by the strong, young men who wanted it for themselves. Elia was now two and used to cry and cry but now only murmured.

Taking leave of her senses Adinah rose up, taking her small baby in her arms and headed for the rubble. Usually it was densely inhabited by guards; some of whom, had ordered the young men to begin building a wall around it. It was beyond curfew but Adinah cared not. In her frailty she found strength, strength for Elia. Waiting she took her chance. The stones seemed to attack her from beneath as she walked and stumbled about blindly, fearfully into darkness. She found a little bunker that created a welcome break from the climb. Breathing sharply she felt the sting of death descending with a faint glory of freedom whispering afar off. She held that whisper within, rocking Elia in abject fear. Her stale breath warm on the baby's pale face.

Anna waiting for Edyta had seen the woman and the baby. Braving the night she came forward to meet her. In silence Adinah passed Anna her baby. She found herself slipping on the rocks beneath her and turned as soldiers and dogs began to appear. Anna disappeared into the woods and Adinah lifting her hands to the bright searchlights was shot.

Fearing the crying baby Anna put her under her coat and lovingly placed her thumb into the little mouth. Shushing and soothing the frightened child she was herself almost paralysed with fear. The dogs were coming quickly as she placed the baby in the barrow and ran to the river. She didn't stop but neither did the dogs.

Mikel had walked all night he was fearful for his friends. Something pervading in his heart had drawn him to set out after them. He walked cold and alone remembering the trails set out by them all in their frequent drills. As he drew near the sense of danger increased; he had not passed his friends on their way back and he knew something was awry. On his approach he heard a whimpering sound and was drawn towards the formerly unseen barrow. Pulling back the blankets he witnessed the young child no more than a baby and clearly Edyta's prize. But where were they? Instinctively he gave the baby trickles of water and began pushing the wheelbarrow homewards. It seemed the only course of action and he didn't want the baby to lead the enemy to their precious home. Leaving his friends behind he strode into the night looking over his shoulder and listening with bated breath at every sound. Heavy in heart but fervent in prayer.

Edyta sat on the grey floor of the public street. She had been spotted aiding the two little girls who sat alone. She knew the Germans were watching her now as she felt inside her coat for her little, gold cross which felt warm and peaceful in her hands. A sharp contrast to her foreboding situation. The guards had cracked the back of her legs with their guns and they felt like jelly when she attempted to stand. At least she was alive. The incessant waiting had given her cause to ruminate unconsciously. She thought about Yosef and about Anna and Mikel but felt this was probably her lot for now and had decided to accept it to release the torture of worry. Committing it to God she closed her mind from the outside and chose to focus on the present time. Day after day she wandered about finding scraps of food and begging a little water from the men at the tap. During the day she trudged to keep warm and at night she needed to get off the streets so stayed in the large hall. Wrapped in her coat, frightened and alone, she couldn't get out! Yet her bread was the Lord now and His promise her strongest hope, her only escape. Internally if not externally.

Security stepped up over the weeks and the soldiers were asking questions and shooting people in the street. The cold briefly splintered by occasional, desperate conversation. It was an evil, incarcerated dump oozing like a great sore amidst the creeping subcultures. A shadow of despair and disillusionment for those without hope. No food, no fires, no heat, no escape. Fear sat in everyone's eyes, the stench increased amid rotting corpses, infestations of rats and disease; all beyond human comprehension. She kept herself to herself as much as possible whilst attempting relationship where she could. There were rumours of resistance but Edyta relied now wholly on the intervention of God to counteract the seeping decline around her.

Some weeks later soldiers began rounding up the Jewish women. Violently and without restraint; Edyta among them. They were bundled into groups or shot to the ground if they protested. Some were just shot anyway. Edyta however was among those herded into stinking, cramped trains and then transported by truck to the death camp. On the journey Edyta took off her cross and prayed for God to cover her as she hid it away. Some of the other woman seemed to eye her suspiciously as if knowing she wasn't one of them. One of these petrified woman managed an embittered smile towards Edyta before being slapped in the face.

Entering the camp room Edyta came face to face with Miriam who seemed to shine like a light in this wretched hovel. Their lives now entwined as they walked towards their given destiny speaking to all, of their beloved Yeshua. The One who saves and saves from darkness into light whatever our circumstance. The One who shines brightly through us in the darkness bringing hope to a lost eternity.

Many years later at a small farmhouse nearby Yosef and his adopted sister shone their lights in a now ravaged land. Dwelling safely with their Uncle Mikel who watched over them and shared stories of the sisters who gave their lives that they may live.

Gerda

... as Gerda passed from this life she grasped the hand of the beautiful lady that shared her food with her and brought news of the Man in white. She'd seen Him herself now, in her dreams. He was alive in her heart despite the shadow of death. This life was passing. She managed to breathe a last word of prayer for the beautiful lady, for strength and then she was gone.

If you do not know Jesus (The Great King) do not miss this section

To enter into eternal life, we only need to believe in Jesus, God's wonderful Son who gave His life for us.

"Greater love has no one than to lay down His life for his friends."
John 15:13

At some point in our lives we will question whether or not there is a God just like Jess. It may be a private undertaking that only we know about or it will be openly seeking through people, prayer, books or perhaps church. Although we may venture to find Him - it will be surprising to find that He is *actually* looking for us!

It reflects in fact, how He is reaching you, *right now*.

As astonishing as that may seem He is seeking all of us, all of the time, to lead us to the truth of who He is and away from the myths and fables surrounding Him.

Jesus died for us.

When He was crucified on that cross the shedding of His blood brought forgiveness for all of our sins. He literally washed us from our sins in His own blood. What a sacrifice of love!

He paid the price for *all* our wrongs and transgressions of which every one of us has fallen short of at some time in our lives, a divine exchange. He wiped the slate clean, completely forgave us as a free gift of love to draw us back to our source, the Father in Heaven. He is always waiting for us to turn, look up, call out and find out who He is. He truly loves us with an everlasting, unchanging love.

Jesus said,
"I am the Door." *John 10:7*
He is the way the truth and the life nobody comes to the

Father except through Him.
John 14:6
This means just what it says. He is the way *through* to the Father in heaven. It is about recognising that He *did* die on the cross for *you* and gave you the free gift of life. The reward for believing in Him and following after Him.

He has set before <u>you</u> an open door and an invitation to eternal life.

If you have been convicted in your heart of this truth you can simply ask Him to come into your life. God says all who call on the name of the Lord will be saved - that name is Jesus.

Ask Jesus into your heart, acknowledge that He is God and that He died on the cross for you, a living sacrifice for everything you have done wrong in your life to completely wash you clean of your past - a fresh start.   The Holy Spirit will make you aware of your sins in order to lead you to repentance.

Just simply say sorry and ask Him to help you turn from this life into the life He had planned for you all along. Jesus forgives once for all and remembers your sin no more. Acknowledge that He rose again after death so that you could be raised to life and enter eternity.

He loves you and will never let you down.

The Bible holds all the truths about Him.
Try getting a genuine copy (New International version or New King James are very good) and starting in the new testament It will be hard going at first but persevere and He will reveal Himself to you. Ask the Holy Spirit to help you understand what you are reading that it His purpose - to reveal truth to you.
Jesus said many will come in His name (pretending to be Him) this is why there are so many sects and lies surrounding the true Jesus, for example Jehovah's Witnesses, Mormons and other manmade cults. This is the devil's master card to

confuse people about the truth.

If you desire to know the real person of Jesus, ask Him.

Torchlight Ministry ~ two strands

Door of Hope: A mentoring ministry for women bringing hope, inner healing, motivation, encouraging faith.

Placing great value in the truth of God's uncompromising Word and taking this out to the world through love, evangelism, authorship and writing.

Jaffa Gate: Recognising Israel's prophetic position. Encouraging prayer and salvation for Jewish people and the importance of Aliyah. Prayer.

Find us on Facebook
Email: torchlight.ministry@gmail.com
WEBSITE: http875.com/

Printed in Great Britain
by Amazon